A-Z
BUSINESS STUDIES
Workbook
Ian Marcousé

Hodder & Stoughton

A MEMBER OF THE HODDER HEADLINE GROUP

Orders: please contact Bookpoint Ltd, 130 Milton Park, Abingdon,
Oxon OX14 4SB. Telephone: (44) 01235 827720, Fax: (44) 01235 400454.
Lines are open from 9.00–6.00, Monday to Saturday, with a 24 hour message
answering service. Email address: orders@bookpoint.co.uk

British Library Cataloguing in Publication Data
A catalogue record for this title is available from the British Library

ISBN 0 340 799811

First published 2002
Impression number   10 9 8 7 6 5 4 3 2 1
Year   2007 2006 2005 2004 2003 2002

Cover artwork by Alan Nanson
Typeset by Florence Production Ltd, Stoodleigh, Devon
Printed in Great Britain for Hodder & Stoughton Educational,
a division of Hodder Headline Plc, 338 Euston Road, London NW1 3BH
by Martins the Printers, Berwick-upon-Tweed

Contents

How to use this book

Welcome to the *A–Z Business Studies Workbook*, a companion to the best-selling *A–Z Handbook*. The *Workbook* provides hundreds of practice exercises, covering the main concepts in AS and A2 Business Studies. The book is designed to be useful from the first day of your business course to the night before your final exam. It is arranged alphabetically, to make it easy for you to look up a term such as 'break-even' and get working straight away.

If, after a lesson, you feel a little unsure about a concept such as elasticity of demand or opportunity cost, the *Workbook* provides questions that start gently, but lead on to quite demanding tasks. All the answers are included at the back of the book, so you can quickly check on your progress. Later, when facing AS or A Level examinations, you can use the special Revision sets of questions for each of the AS and A Level module exams.

The entries start with a 'fill in the missing words' section. This may seem a bit too easy, but its function is to help remind you of precise definitions of the relevant business terms. If you think carefully about these precise definitions, you will be in a much stronger position to answer the questions that follow. Throughout the *Workbook* many of the questions are quite testing. They are trying to make sure that you understand each concept really well, and that you can apply it to different business situations. This can help you to gain the marks for understanding and application that represent up to two thirds of the marks on business exam papers.

When checking numerical answers, do take time over any answer you get wrong. Where did you slip up and why? With written answers, please do not worry if your answers differ from those provided. There are often plenty of possible correct answers to business questions, so your answers are not necessarily wrong just because they are different from mine.

My students have tried out most of the enclosed questions, and found them testing but very helpful in building confidence in the underlying theory of the subject. I very much hope you find them of equal value.

Acknowledgements

Many thanks to Tim Gregson-Williams and Alexia Chan at Hodder & Stoughton, to Roger Raymond (for spotting some cash flow flaws) and to my wonderful AS and A2 students at Lambeth College.

Ian Marcousé
AS/A2 Business Studies Chief Examiner

Contents by Subject Area

A–Z Questions

Accountability, authority and responsibility

A Missing words

.... is power that has been delegated down an organisation's
hierarchy. The employee to whom the power is delegated is then ....
to his/her boss for success or failure. The employee may be held to account if things
go wrong. Nevertheless the .... for success or failure lies
with the boss who delegated the power. Responsibility cannot be delegated, only
authority.

B Briefly explain why

1 'Responsibility cannot be delegated, only authority'. ....

....

....

2 Accountability may be weakened if staff are answerable to more than one boss.

....

....

....

3 The delegation of authority to make decisions must be supplemented by authority over
budgets and spending.

....

....

....

C Analysing data

Look at this diagram of an organisational hierarchy, then answer the questions below:

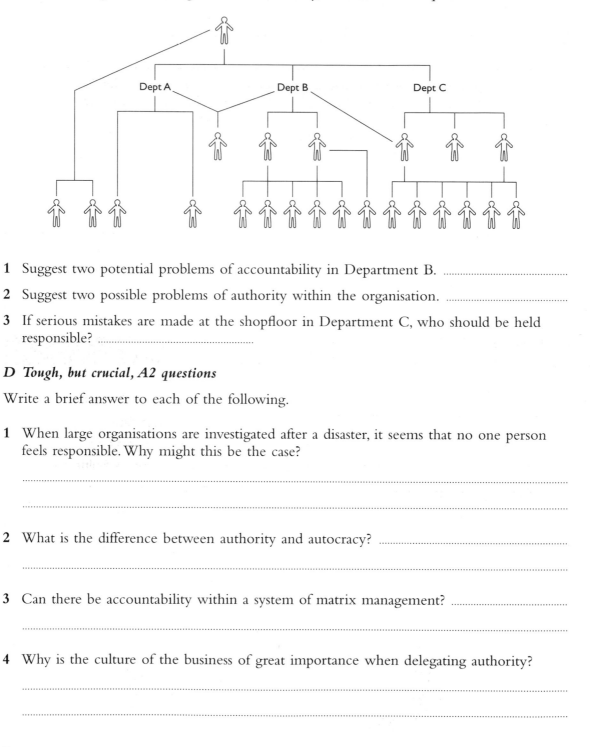

1 Suggest two potential problems of accountability in Department B. ....

2 Suggest two possible problems of authority within the organisation. ....

3 If serious mistakes are made at the shopfloor in Department C, who should be held responsible? ....

D Tough, but crucial, A2 questions

Write a brief answer to each of the following.

1 When large organisations are investigated after a disaster, it seems that no one person feels responsible. Why might this be the case?

....

....

2 What is the difference between authority and autocracy? ....

....

3 Can there be accountability within a system of matrix management? ....

....

4 Why is the culture of the business of great importance when delegating authority?

....

....

Adding value

A Missing words

Adding value means creating a finished product that is worth more to the customer than the sum of the parts.

> At Starbucks, 25p of coffee beans, milk and flavourings turns into a selling price of £2 or more. The £ .... of value added pays for staff, the equipment, the sofas, the rent and still generates a generous .... Adding value is the ultimate goal of Research and Development teams and marketing departments. It generates the surplus that pays the bills.
>
> The formula for calculating value added is:
>
> .... — bought-in goods and services

B Ways to add value

Match each product type with possible ways to add value.

Product type	Ways to add value
1 Car manufacturing	a) Obtain a prestigious address b) Measure up, then make to fit
2 Biscuit production	c) Offer a short lead time d) Add a technical innovation e) Carry out the process faultlessly
3 Running a private hospital	f) Excellent design and styling g) Impressive, prestige packaging
4 Making wedding dresses	h) Use low-cost materials where they're not visible to the customer

C Calculations

1   Tardew Car Dealers buys a 6-year-old Fiesta for £700 cash. One car seat is replaced and a new exhaust fitted – the parts cost £105. After a thorough clean-up inside and out and a squirt of air freshener inside (materials cost £5), the Fiesta goes onto the forecourt at £1,495 and is sold for £1,400 a week later.

a) Calculate the added value. ....

b) Explain why this added value cannot be treated as pure profit.

....

....

2   *Strength* is a cure for baldness based on herbal medicines. It sells in bottles priced at £24 that provide sufficient for two weeks. A full cure is said to take one year, though the packaging says that only 50% of users will find the cure effective. Jenny Ireland, the inventor of *Strength*, has hired a well-known TV and film actor to promote the product on a series of TV commercials. The production process and costs of *Strength* are a closely guarded secret, but the materials themselves cost no more than 30p – the same as the packaging. Jenny often refers to the 'huge overheads' of running the business, but with sales of 15 million bottles last year, no wonder she has just bought herself a Mercedes sports car.

a) Calculate the:
   i)   value added per bottle. ....
   ii) value added as a % of materials costs. ....
   iii) total value added in the last year. ....

b) Give two justifications Jenny might find to defend the high price she charges for *Strength*.

....

....

D Explain why

1   A unique selling point is a very effective way of adding value.

....

....

2   Modern manufacturers say that the best way to add value is good design.

....

....

Aims and objectives

A Missing words

> Business success relies upon a clear vision of the .... (goal/role) being pursued. The starting point is to agree on the ...., which present the goals in a general way. To achieve these general aims, it helps to set ...., which are more precise targets of what should be achieved and when. A strategy can then be agreed on how best to achieve the ....

The logical order, then, is:

AIMS
↓
OBJECTIVES
↓
STRATEGY

B Theory into practice

> A student was asked about her aims and objectives. She replied: 'My aim is to be rich and my objective is to make my first £250,000 by the time I'm 25.'

1 a) Identify two features of her objective that make it more likely to be effective.

....

....

b) Which of the following seem plausible strategies for achieving her objective?

i) Go to university, get a top-class degree, than get a well-paid job in the City of London.

ii) Leave school at 18 and open a retail business with the potential for many branches nationally.

iii) Leave school and get a job as a trainee manager for Barclays Bank.

Answer ....

C Data response question

S. Davis Ltd is a web-based travel agent owned by two brothers that has grown hugely in the past two years. The staff level has risen from 11 to 92 and the number of customers from 213 to 1,143!

Suggest three ways in which S. Davis Ltd might benefit from clear aims and objectives.

1 ....

2 ....

3 ....

D Place an A (aim), an O (objective) or an S (strategy) by each of the following statements

1 To diversify our business.

2 To make home-delivery, authentic Italian pizza available to every home in Britain.

3 To allocate £400,000 to developing a brand new website.

4 To increase market share to 8% by the end of next year.

5 To achieve brand awareness among the majority of the target market within three months.

6 To finance growth by using credit factoring.

7 To get promotion to the Premiership within five years.

Examiners' Notes

Good analysis comes from knowing the subtle differences between concepts; so don't use aims and objectives interchangeably – make it clear that you know the differences between them.

Ansoff's matrix

A Missing words

Igor Ansoff was an expert on business strategy whose views on risk can be presented graphically as Ansoff's matrix. This places a firm's products on a grid that sets the level of novelty of the product being launched against the novelty of the .... being entered. Ansoff said that the safest strategy is to stick to developing familiar p... within a familiar marketplace, e.g. Persil with 'new improved' detergents. The riskiest is to launch a brand new product into a market where the business has no prior experience. The latter approach he called d... .

B Explain why

1 Brand new, innovative products are riskier to launch than very familiar ones.

....

....

2 Ansoff believed that – if successful – high-risk projects yield the highest rewards.

....

....

3 There is a high failure rate among successful British retailers who have set up in America.

....

....

C Data response

Place each of these products onto the Virgin Group matrix shown on p. 8. Assume Richard Branson ran Virgin Atlantic only before the following ideas came about.

1 The 1994 launch of Virgin Cola.

2 The 1995 launch of Virgin Direct (financial services).

3 The 1996 launch of Virgin Express (low-cost European airline).

4 The 1996 launch of Virgin Trains.

5 The 1999 launch of Virgin Mobile (phones).

6 The 2000 launch of Virgin Blue (low-cost Australian airline).

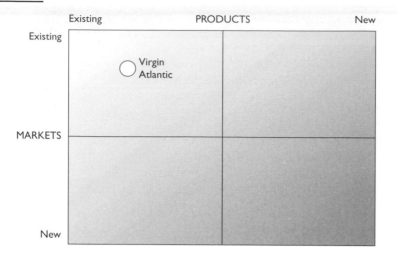

D Successful strategy based on Ansoff

Draw arrows to show which action or actions match the strategies listed on the left.

Strategy	Implications or actions
1 Easyjet launching Easyrentacar	a) Given the huge risks, keep financially strong by starting with a low-geared, strong balance sheet
2 Marriott Hotels buying up Meridien Hotels	b) With low-risk product development, heavy investment on advertising can be afforded
3 A small clothes shop opening a medium-sized clothing factory	c) With no risks being taken on the marketing side, the business can afford riskier finances, e.g. high gearing
4 Heinz sticking closely to its dominant profit centres: beans, soups and sauces	d) Although market knowledge will not be a problem, different workplace cultures may cause risks to managers

Examiners' **Notes**

Remember that Ansoff was interested in strategy in relation to *risk*. He was not telling companies to avoid risk; he wanted them to be aware of the risks they were taking.

Assets employed

A Missing words

Assets employed comprises two elements: .... (assets needed over the medium to long term) and working .... (also known as net current assets). On a balance sheet, assets employed always equals .... employed. In published accounts, assets employed is described as 'total assets less current liabilities'.

B Which of the following formulae are correct?

1 **a)** Assets employed = fixed assets + (current assets − current liabilities)
  b) Assets employed = fixed assets + current assets
  c) Assets employed = total assets − current liabilities
  d) Assets employed = capital employed   *Answer* ....

C Calculate assets employed in the following cases

1 Stocks £20,000; property £80,000; overdraft £15,000; debtors £40,000; cash £5,000

....

2 Fixed assets £40,000; current assets £55,000; current liabilities £50,000; loans £10,000

....

D Missing words

Use words from the following list to fill in the gaps in the balance sheet. Calculate the missing totals.

	£000
Fixed assets	1,100
Stock	450
Debtors	220
Cash	160
Current liabilities	620
1	....
2	....
Loans	710
Share capital	50
Reserves	550
3	....

capital employed

assets employed

working capital

Average rate of return (ARR)

A Missing words

The average rate of return is the average annual .... profit made over the lifetime of an investment. It is found by calculating the total profit on the investment, dividing it by the number of years of life, then taking that figure as a percentage of the initial .... The resulting figure (the percentage ARR) can then be compared with the general interest rate to help decide whether the investment is worth the ....

B Which of the following are advantages of the ARR method of investment appraisal?

1 Shows how quickly the investment is recovered. ....

2 Shows the profitability of the investment. ....

3 Can appraise investments of different sizes. ....

4 Based on estimates of future cash flows. ....

C Calculate

1 The average rate of return from the following data

	Net cash flow	Cumulative cash
NOW	(£200,000)	(£200,000)
Year 1	£80,000	(£120,000)
Year 2	£110,000	(£10,000)
Year 3	£120,000	£110,000
Year 4	£50,000	£160,000

Answer ....

2   A double-glazing firm has a policy of only investing in projects that yield an ARR of at least 15%.

   a) What is the term given for a policy such as this? ....

   b) Does the following project deliver sufficiently high returns?

	Cash in	Cash out
NOW	–	£60,000
Year 1	£240,000	£240,000
Year 2	£360,000	£300,000
Year 3	£320,000	£275,000

....

....

D Outline two

1   Advantages of ARR compared with the pay-back method of appraising investments.

....

....

....

2   Reasons why ARR should be used together with pay-back, rather than on its own.

....

....

....

E True or false?

Place an F or a T by each of the following statements.

1   An ARR of 25% is a poor rate of return, as you're only getting a quarter of your money back.

2   An ARR of 33% is terrific, as you'll double your money in three years.

3   An ARR of 16% is fine if interest rates are at 6%.

Balance sheet 1

A Missing words

A balance sheet is a listing of all a firm's .... and ....
at a point in .... It balances because double entry bookkeeping ensures
that assets always equal liabilities. Specifically, assets employed equals
.... employed.

A balance sheet has three main sections: .... assets are the long-term
assets such as property and machinery. W........................... capital shows the short-
term assets (minus the short-term liabilities). These two sections, added together,
comprise the .... employed. This total is balanced by the loans and
shareholders' funds that comprise the firm's capital employed.

Here is a summary of the above:

fixed assets	+ working capital	=	assets employed
			=
loans	+ shareholders' funds	=	capital employed

B Circle the odd one out along each row

1 Current assets: Creditors   Debtors   Work in progress   Cash

2 Current liabilities: Tax due   Overdraft   Creditors   Old stock

3 Capital employed: Reserves   5-year loan   Cash   Share capital

4 Fixed assets: Vehicles   Fixtures and fittings   Stock   Property

C Insert the five missing terms into the following balance sheet

	£000
{Property	140
{Vehicles	110
{Stock	55
{Debtors and cash	70
{Creditors	65
{Overdraft	90
Net Current Assets	(30)
(.................... ....)	
Assets employed	**220**
Loans	105
{Share capital	25
{Reserves	90
Capital employed	**220**

1 ....

2 ....

3 ....

4

5 ....

D Balance sheet construction

Reconstruct BW Co.'s balance sheet from the following:

Stock £40,000, creditors £25,000, debtors £40,000, property £150,000,
loans £65,000, cash £20,000, share capital £10,000, reserves £150,000.

Make sure you provide totals for working capital, assets employed and capital employed.

Balance sheet 2 (including ratios)

A Circle the odd one out

1 Stock	Creditors	Debtors	Cash
2 Share capital	Cash	Reserves	Loans
3 Machinery	Property	Goodwill	Fixtures and fittings
4 Dividend yield	Return on capital	Acid test	Gearing

B Missing words

1 To measure a company's liquidity the .... test ratio is helpful. It shows how able the firm is to meet its short-term ....

2 On a balance sheet, assets employed balances with .... employed. The assets employed (top) section of the balance sheet shows how the firm's capital has been ....

3 .... measures how dependent a firm is on borrowed money. High .... suggests that the firm's finances are relatively risky.

C Calculations

	£000
Fixed assets	160
Stock	80
Debtors	45
Cash	25
Current liabilities	140

1 Look at this balance sheet extract for a company with annual sales of £365,000.

a) Calculate the acid test ratio. ....

b) Calculate the firm's assets employed. ....

c) Calculate the credit period taken by the average customer. State any assumption you have made. ....

2 If a firm with £30,000 of stock has a stock turnover of six times and a gross profit margin of 50%, what is its annual sales turnover?

....

....

Break-even analysis

A Add to the XYZ break-even chart

1 **a)** the total costs line

   b) labelling of the horizontal axis

   c) the break-even point and the safety margin (if sales are 2,250 units)

   d) the profit/loss if only 1,000 units are sold.

B From the XYZ chart, calculate

1 **a)** the selling price of the company's products ....

   b) the precise break-even point ....

   c) the profit at full capacity. ....

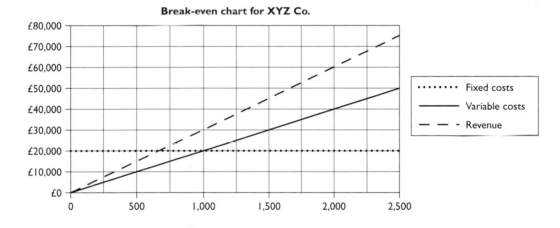

Break-even chart for XYZ Co.

Fixed costs
Variable costs
Revenue

C State two assumptions made in break-even charts such as the above.

....

....

D The BN Co. has

- fixed costs of £160,000
- selling price £9
- variable costs of £5 per unit
- demand for 50,000 units

Calculate:

1 **a)** the existing profit ....

   b) the change in profit if a £1 price cut boosts demand by 10% ....

E Draw a break-even chart to show

- fixed costs £200,000
- selling price £2.50
- variable costs £0.90 per unit
- maximum capacity 180,000 units

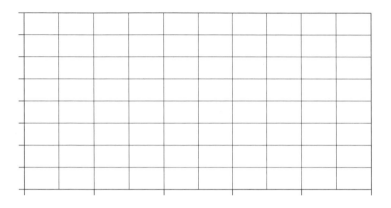

Mark and state the profit and safety margin if demand is for 150,000 units.

....

Budgeting

A Missing words

Budgeting means making an estimate of the appropriate level of revenues or .... over a future period of time. Budgets usually cover monthly periods and are often set 12 months in advance. .... budgets need to be achieved or exceeded in order to meet a firm's revenue objectives. .... budgets need to be met or .... so that total costs are kept low enough to ensure the planned level of profit.

B Setting budgets

True or false?

1 Many organisations set budgets based on the last year's figures plus inflation. ☐

2 Managers will always attempt to set sales budgets quite low and cost budgets quite high. ☐

3 Zero budgeting is when a firm decides to scrap its budgeting system altogether. ☐

4 Budgets set by senior managers will demotivate if junior managers think they cannot be met. ☐

C Which terms are defined by the following statements?

1 The difference between budgeted and actual figures.

....

2 Setting budgets at £0 to force managers to justify every £ of budget they seek.

....

3 When actual figures produce less profit than the budgeted ones.

....

D Calculations

Calculate the missing figures for **a–k**.

All figures in £000s	July			August		
	Budget	Actual	Variance	Budget	Actual	Variance
Revenue	245	230	b)	310	315	g) ....
Materials	120	115	c)	145	155	h) ....
Other variable costs	30	30	d)	40	45	i) ....
Fixed overheads	65	65	e)	65	70	j) ....
Profit	30	a)	f)	60	45	k) ....

E Data response

Staton Ltd was an underperforming pet supplies wholesaler. Staff morale was low and revenues barely covered costs. A new manager decided to introduce a budgeting system for all departments. He set sales and cost targets for the coming 12 months and introduced a bonus scheme that gave a 10% salary bonus for department managers who beat their targets. At two of the seven departments the managers worked hard for a while, then relaxed when they were sure their targets would be beaten. The other five managers reacted badly from the start and the two best-regarded left for other jobs within 8 weeks. By the end of the year, Staton Ltd was making significant losses.

1 Outline one key mistake made by Staton Ltd's new manager.

....

2 How might staff within a department feel about a bonus being given solely to the manager?

....

3 Briefly outline four lessons this short case can provide about the importance of taking great care when setting up a budget system.

a) ....

b) ....

c) ....

d) ....

Business cycle

A Missing words

> The business (or t............................) cycle is the tendency in free m............................
> economies for demand and output to move up and down in a wave-like motion.
> Between 1946 and 1981, this cycle lasted for about .... years; in other
> words from the peak to the trough was about two and a half years and the upturn
> lasted for about the same time. Fortunately, because the underlying trend in demand
> was moving ahead quite rapidly, the upturns were sharp and the downturns quite
> minor. Since 1980/81, the dreadful recession of 1990/91 and the apparent downturn
> in 2001 suggest that the business cycle now spans ten-year periods.

B Cause or effect?

Put a C, an E or both by the following, depending on whether they are a probable cause or effect of recessions.

1 Deliberate destocking by firms ....

2 Sharp rise in interest rates ....

3 Rationalisation programmes undertaken by firms ....

4 Excess business investment leading to saturation ....

5 Cutbacks in consumer spending ....

6 Government anti-inflationary policies ....

7 Rising demand for 'inferior' goods ....

8 Cutbacks in spending on durables and luxuries ....

C *Explain why*

1 Firms' cash flow can deteriorate rapidly in an economic downturn.

....

....

2 The timing of recessions is very hard to predict.

....

....

....

3 Firms prefer long, steady upturns to sharp, rapid ones.

....

D *What happens in which phase of the cycle?*

For each of the following, write down the letter(s) of the characteristic(s) of that particular phase of the business cycle.

1 Slump ....

2 Upturn ....

3 Boom ....

4 Recession/downturn ....

a) Rising wage and price inflation	w) Many new business start-ups
b) Business investment low, but not falling	x) Interest rates falling
c) Firms may be building up stock levels	y) Unemployment becoming uncomfortably high
d) Imports may be rising rapidly	z) Growth, but no sign of inflation yet

E *Data response*

Kafton Ltd makes fork-lift trucks. Demand has been slipping in recent years, but the last three months has seen a dramatic downturn. There has been much talk of recession in the media, and Kafton's regular customers make it clear that they are delaying orders while they 'wait and see'. Now Joe Kafton needs to decide whether to carry out a staff cutback or not. He is very reluctant as many staff have over 10 years' service, but the company has made large losses in the last three months, and Joe is worried about the effects on the company's long-term future.

1 Why may it be too early to be sure a recession is under way?

....

2 What problems may Kafton suffer if the cutbacks are postponed, but it does prove to be a recession?

....

....

3 In a recession, either shareholders or staff are likely to suffer (or both). Outline the case for Kafton to protect its staff as much as possible.

....

....

....

Business organisations

A Missing words

Business organisations include unlimited .... businesses such as sole .... and limited liability (i..............................) companies such as .... limited companies (Ltd) and .... limited companies (plcs). The most important distinction is whether or not an organisation has limited liability. If so, the business becomes a company that is a separate legal entity from its .... (its owners). This provides legal and financial protection that can give the owners the confidence to take commercial risks without fear of ruining their family finances.

B True or false?

Place an F or a T by each of the following statements.

1 Only public limited companies are allowed to advertise to raise capital by issuing more shares. ☐

2 It is riskier to give credit to a sole trader than to a private limited company. ☐

3 To set up a private limited company you must apply to Companies House for incorporation. ☐

4 A limited business is not liable for its own losses. ☐

5 The most common form of business in the UK is the sole trader. ☐

C *Which characteristic matches which business?*

For each of the following, write down the letter(s) of the characteristic(s) which match that particular business.

1 Private limited company ....

2 Public limited company ....

3 Sole trader ....

4 None of these ....

---

a) Detailed accounts must be published, plus a Chairman's statement and an auditor's report

b) Up to 20 people can work together, all with unlimited liability

c) Must always state Ltd after its name

d) Can be started with as little as £100 of share capital

w) May be difficult to have family holidays due to concern over who can be trusted to run the business

x) Can be started today, without any formalities or paperwork

y) Must always state plc after its name

z) Is owned by the government on behalf of the general public

---

Examiners' **Notes**

Think about this: small, unlimited liability businesses are the riskiest to own but the safest to deal with; small, limited liability companies are the safest to own but the riskiest to deal with. Can you see why?

Business plan

A Missing words

The owners of .... firms often make decisions with little discussion and little formality. The implications may be thought through (and some back-of-the-envelope calculations done), but the decisions remain largely based on .... (hunch/lunch). A business plan is a document with a set structure that encourages a firm to detail its objectives, plus its strategy and detailed plans for meeting them. These would include a .... forecast, a profit projection, a marketing plan and an assessment of the staffing and operational implications.

B Draw arrows to match the elements of the plan (on the left) to the outcomes (on the right)

Element	Outcome
1 Workforce plan	a) Shows the sales volume (or value) needed to cover all costs
2 Cash flow forecast	b) Identifies the target market, the promotional budget and how it is to be spent
3 Marketing plan	c) Estimates the amount of capital required, how it is to be raised and how it is to be repaid
4 Financing proposals	d) Estimates the revenue and costs anticipated over the lifetime of the proposal
5 Break-even analysis	e) Identifies the number and type of skills needed to achieve output and sales targets
6 Profit forecast	f) Predicts money coming into and out of the firm's bank account

C Give two reasons why

1 Many businesses only construct business plans if they have to (for a bank, for instance).

....

....

2   Banks are sceptical of the financial data presented in a business plan.

    ....

    ....

    ....

3   A well prepared business plan may help a business avoid serious mistakes.

    ....

    ....

    ....

D True or false?

Place a T or an F by each of the following statements.

1   Business plans are pointless because reality never works out to be the same as the plan.

2   Most businesses do not need a business plan as they never raise any external share or loan capital.

3   The hardest part of any business plan is estimating the amount and timing of customer revenues.

4   The value of the plan is largely to force the director(s) to think about the overall implications of a decision, i.e. not only the financial impact but also the marketing, staffing and operational effects.

E Good plan or bad plan?

State whether each of the following represents a good business plan or not, giving your reasons.

1   Two sheets setting out briefly the aim, the competition, the market gap, the idea and the resources needed.

    ....

    ....

2   A twenty-page Lloyds Bank Business Plan, filled out to show the detailed expectations about costs, revenues, cash flows, loan requirements and loan repayments.

    ....

    ....

Capacity utilisation and intensity

A Missing words

Capacity is the v............................. of output a firm is capable of producing. Capacity utilisation measures actual output as a percentage of the firm's capability. If the maximum capacity is 10,000 units a month and the actual output is 6,500 units, capacity utilisation is ....%. As fixed (o.............................) costs are related to maximum capacity, if the firm has low capacity utilisation, its fixed costs per unit will be .... and so too will be its average total costs per unit.

Capital intensity raises a separate issue. To what extent are the total costs of the business weighted towards fixed capital (such as machinery)? Or is the business labour intensive, i.e. labour costs form a high proportion of total costs? The former case is more likely to be true of large firms (especially in the manufacturing sector) whereas the labour-intensive firms are more likely to be .... firms especially in the .... sector.

B True or false?

Place an F or a T by each of the following statements.

1 Low capacity utilisation means low unit costs. ☐

2 Low capital intensity means high labour costs per unit. ☐

3 High labour intensity may mean high costs but high flexibility and good customer service. ☐

4 High capacity utilisation keeps unit costs down as machinery and staff are being used productively. ☐

5 An increase in capital intensity might lead to redundancies. ☐

C Calculations

1 Six months ago, John Collins started up a retail business with overheads of £4,000 per week, including £900 on staff, £700 on rent and the rest on the cost of leasing a state-of-the-art automated supply system. This enables customers to order over the phone, the internet or in person, and a robotic stock-picking system finds the item and delivers it to a collection bay. Current unit sales of 7,200 per week are close to the system's maximum capacity of 8,000 units.

a) Calculate the firm's % capacity utilisation.

....

b) Calculate the capital intensity of John Collins' business.

....

c) A rival retailer has a labour intensity of 70%. Identify one advantage and one disadvantage to John Collins of its capital intensity.

....

....

2   JT Co.'s fixed overheads of £600,000 a month pay for a maximum capacity of 200,000 units. Variable costs are £2 per unit, the selling price is £8 and current demand is for 120,000 units.

a) What is JT Co.'s capacity utilisation?

....

b) Calculate JT Co.'s fixed costs per unit at 120,000 units and at maximum capacity.

....

c) Explain how the above data enable you to know that JT Co.'s profit margin is £1 per unit at sales of 120,000 units, but £3 per unit at maximum capacity.

....

....

d) Calculate the % increase in the firm's total profit that would result from a sales increase from 120,000 to 200,000 units.

....

....

Examiners' **Notes**

The concepts of capacity utilisation and intensity are crucial to cost effective production; be sure to understand their differences and then practise using them in homework answers. They offer huge scope for improving analysis marks.

Capital and revenue expenditure

A Missing words

Capital expenditure is spending on .... assets such as property, machinery and vehicles. It is investment spending on assets that should yield benefits for many years to come. Because of this, capital spending is accounted for through depreciation, which spreads the cost of an asset over its expected useful .... Revenue spending, by contrast, is on current items that must be charged in full against the current year's revenue, e.g. wages, bought-in .... and expenses such as electricity, ... and advertising. So the key accounting difference is that £1 million spent on advertising will be charged in full as a cost in this year's accounts. £1 million on machinery expected to last 5 years will be charged as £200,000 a year for each of the 5 years.

B True or false?

Place a T or an F by each of the following statements.

1 Capital spending takes time to yield benefits, while revenue spending generates the products that can be sold today.

2 As freehold property does not depreciate, £50 million spent on land would not be recorded as a cost in a firm's accounts.

3 Revenue spending always generates revenue, such as spending on raw materials.

4 Government capital spending includes spending on roads, hospitals and military equipment.

C Identify the effect

1 On a firm's balance sheet of a decision to double the depreciation rate on machinery.

2 On a firm's P and L account of a decision to depreciate a £100,000 computer system over four years.

3 On a firm's long-term competitiveness of a decision to cut back on capital spending.

4 On a firm's balance sheet of a decision to depreciate £500,000 of production robots over ten years instead of five.

Cash flow

A Missing words

Cash flow is the movement of cash into and out of a business. In this sense, cash means not only notes and coins but also credit payments such as by cheque or credit card. Therefore it is best understood as the movement of cash in and out of a firm's bank account.

> The key measures of cash flow are a) the cash balance, i.e. how much cash (or overdraft) the firm has and b) the net cash flow, which is cash in *minus* cash .... over a period of time, usually a ....

B Identify the brand name formed by the first letter of each of the following terms

1   When a customer proves unable to pay a bill, perhaps due to liquidation.

   ....

2   Items that can be sold to generate cash. ....

3   When a firm sells a property freehold but simultaneously leases it for a term of, perhaps, 20 years. ....

4   Using a banking service that obtains payment from customers – for a fee.

   ....

   Answer ....

C Cash flow and growth

1   Identify two ways that rapid growth can hit a firm's cash flow.

   ....

   ....

2   If a firm chooses to boost its sales by offering interest-free credit, what will be the effect on its cash flow?

   ....

   ....

3   To finance rapid growth, firms can use credit factoring; explain its effects on cash flow.

   ....

   ....

D Data response

Bandul Nursery sells plants and flowers. Its cash flow forecast for the spring sales period is shown below.

	February	March	April	May
Cash at start	£45,000	£50,000	e)	h) ....
Cash inflow	£85,000	£115,000	f)	£110,000
Cash outflow	£80,000	c)	£100,000	£95,000
Net cash flow	a)	d)	£25,000	i) ....
Cumulative cash	b)	£75,000	g)	j) ....

1 Fill in the gaps **a–j**.

2 In June, Bandul is planning to purchase an acre of land next to the nursery for £170,000. Outline:

   a) the effect on Bandul's cumulative cash position

   ....

   b) what they might do to improve their cash flow position.

   ....

   ....

   ....

E Outline two

1 Difficulties a travel agent would face in forecasting cash flows accurately.

   ....

   ....

2 Risks that a firm faces if it regularly operates in the red, i.e. financed by an overdraft.

   ....

   ....

Communication

A Missing words

Internal communication within any organisation must be effective to ensure that staff share a sense of purpose about the g............................ and strategies being pursued. It is also vital for efficiency, as perceived by outside stakeholders such as c................................... , shareholders and suppliers. For if messages are not passed on and responded to, complaints or suggestions from outside may be unanswered. Problems of communication are widespread and should not be underestimated. They are made worse if there are many i............................... through whom messages must pass. As communication difficulties tend to be a bigger and costlier problem in bigger businesses, they represent a major .... of scale.

B Match the problem to the consequence

Draw arrows to connect each communication problem to its probable consequence to the business.

Communication problem	Business consequence
1 Over-reliance on written communication	a) Directors may not understand shopfloor problems and feelings
2 Low staff morale	b) Communication may be one-way, impersonal and demotivating
3 Many layers of hierarchy	c) Stressful to feel unable to answer every query adequately
4 Lack of common language	d) May be too much communication and may be too impersonal
5 Communication overload	e) Professional staff such as scientists may explain a problem, but its importance might not be understood by managers
6 Over-reliance on e-mail	f) Staff may lack the motivation to listen or respond

C Identify two

1 Barriers to effective communication.

....

....

2 Reasons why feedback is important to effective communication.

....

....

3 Possible solutions to poor communications in large firms.

....

4 Effects of poor communications upon morale.

....

....

D Data response

Buskin Ltd is a small, struggling firm with about 80 staff. Since Jenny B. (owner and chief executive) made 12 staff redundant, the remaining staff have made no secret of their dislike and distrust of their boss. Jenny B. has responded by keeping her door firmly shut and dealing with staff indirectly, through her secretary.

Last week, a major client company closed its account following a mix-up in which 4,000 signs saying 'Toilet' were delivered instead of 400 signs saying 'To let'. This has led to a verbal warning of dismissal being given to Bob Ware, who protests that he just did as he was told.

1 Explain why it may be a problem to communicate 'with staff indirectly'.

....

....

2 Briefly outline what you think Jenny B. should do next, to try to improve the situation.

....

....

....

....

Examiners' Notes

Exam students like to suggest that lots of communication is desirable. In fact, too many e-mails, memos or newsletters detract from important or urgent issues. The key is usually to have direct communication of important issues, with plenty of scope for direct feedback.

Constraints (internal and external)

A Missing words

Constraints are factors that can prevent a firm from achieving its
.... Well-managed firms think ahead to anticipate likely
internal constraints such as lack of finance, too few staff or insufficiently strong
brand names. What is harder is to plan for .... constraints such as an
economic downturn, a sharp rise in the £ or a major .... group
campaign. Ideally, firms should bear constraints in mind when setting their
objectives. In some cases they may set less ambitious goals; in other circumstances
they may deliberately plan to break through a .... Sometimes these
constraints are self imposed, such as Mercedes avoiding building small cars until the
1990s, when they developed the Smart car and the A Class.

B Internal, external or nothing?

Put an I (internal), an E (external) or an N (nothing) by each of the following.

1 Shortage of skilled labour ☐   6 Sharp rise in interest rates ☐

2 Rise in market share ☐   7 New competitor enters market ☐

3 Fall in consumer confidence ☐   8 Setting profit goal of £1 million ☐

4 Rise in price of raw materials ☐   9 No spare capacity ☐

5 Firm has high level of debt ☐

C What might a firm do?

State briefly how a firm might tackle each of these constraints.

1 Insufficient working capital to launch a new product.

....

....

2 Cannot retain skilled IT staff.

....

....

3 Oil of Olay has a promising, youth-focused new product, but an 'old' brand image.

....

....

....

D Match the constraint to the objective

Draw arrows to show which constraint threatens which objective.

Objective	Constraint
1 Profit increase by 40% to £4 million this year	**a)** Strong brand image has validity only for one product
2 Boost market share from 17% to 22% this year	**b)** A recession may change consumer buying habits
3 Re-launch products to make them more upmarket	**c)** Staff demand pay rises to share in the firm's success
4 Marlboro wants to diversify into snack foods	**d)** A major new competitor breaks into the market

E Internalising external constraints

All firms want to bring external constraints within their own control; how might a firm attempt to achieve this in each of the following cases?

1 Threats of protests over child labour used by a Vietnamese supplier.

....

....

2 Reduce vulnerability to a high value of the £.

....

....

3 Reduce vulnerability to a price war started by competitors.

....

....

Examiners' Notes

Distinguish carefully between constraints that cannot be overcome and those that should be treated as an opportunity to show leadership, innovative thinking and to outstrip your competition.

Contribution

A Missing words

Contribution is the surplus generated over variable costs when selling one or more products. It can be measured per unit, using the formula: price − .... cost per unit = contribution per unit. This shows how much each sale contributes to covering the fixed overheads of the business. It can also be looked at in total, i.e. total contribution (contribution per unit × quantity sold). This can be a useful short-cut to calculating .... , as total contribution − fixed overheads = ...

B True or false?

Place an F or a T by each of the following statements.

1 Contribution per unit is the same as gross profit per unit. ☐

2 Contribution per unit can be increased by cutting variable costs. ☐

3 A price cut may cut contribution but boost net profit. ☐

4 A price rise will boost contribution and therefore will boost net profit. ☐

C Calculations

1 A firm with variable costs of 40p per unit has sales of 6,000 units at £2 each. The fixed costs are £4,000.

    a) Calculate contribution per unit. ....

    b) Calculate the number of units needed to break even. ....

    c) Calculate the firm's profit. ....

2 Using the contribution method, calculate a firm's profit before and after the following.

Before: A product sold for £2 has variable costs of 80p per unit. Demand is for 50,000 units and fixed costs are £15,000.

After: Then the firm decides to cut price by 20p, causing sales to rise to 56,000 units.

    a) Profit before ....

    b) Profit after ....

    c) If the objective was to boost profit, should the firm have done it? ....

Cost and profit centres

A Missing word

Large businesses may have 20,000 staff and spend £500 million a year on costs. Therefore no one person can approve or direct every £ of spending. It becomes essential to .... spending power to middle or junior managers. To do this, the business can notionally be divided into small units, each acting as a small business with its own profit and loss account. Then the senior managers can merely monitor the progress of the profit centre 'directors'. Cost centres are only responsible for meeting their own cost targets, but profit centres are responsible for their revenues (and therefore profit) as well.

B True or false?

Place a T or an F by each of the following statements.

1 In very large firms, staff may find it hard to see how their own efforts can affect overall performance. ☐

2 Profit centres focus the most profitable products on particular managers or departments. ☐

3 Delegating spending power requires huge trust and should be matched by high quality training. ☐

4 Without cost centres, firms often rely on departmental budgets that allow past spending to continue into the future. ☐

5 Linked spreadsheets allow the Finance Director to build a whole picture from all the individual cost/profit centres. ☐

C Match the pros and cons to the correct budgeting approach

Complete the following using the information on p. 35.

1 Cost centres   Pros: .... Cons: ....

2 Budgets for each department   Pros: .... Cons: ....

3 All expenditure requires approval from the finance director   Pros: .... Cons: ....

4 Profit centres   Pros: .... Cons: ....

Pros or Cons	Pros or Cons
a) Profit sharing can be localised to increase incentive effects	v) Bureaucratic to calculate costs and revenues between departments
b) Costs can be controlled rigorously	w) Departments inflate budget requests to make targets easy to get
c) Decision making is localised and may therefore be better	x) Ensures that all spending is channelled towards the same goal
d) Decision making may be slow and may be ill-informed	y) Highly motivating to be given the resources to achieve your goals
e) No incentive to minimise costs	z) With no measured revenues, customer needs may be ignored

D Risks with cost and profit centres

Fill in the missing words.

1 Excess focus on targets may lead local managers to take ....-.......................... decisions, e.g. price promotions.

2 May be hard to identify every cost that is generated by a department, therefore staff may minimise costs that are allocated to them, but do nothing about .... costs such as telephone or heating bills.

3 Focus upon financial performance may divert attention from issues of social .... that may suddenly become all-important, such as passenger safety on the railways or clean air around a factory.

Examiners' Notes

Although important for controlling costs and boosting profit, the key purpose of cost and profit centres is a managerial one: to enable effective delegation to take place. It would be useful to look up delegation in the *Complete A–Z Handbook of Business Studies*.

Costs

A Missing words

Businesses analyse their costs in many ways.

They usually start by identifying the costs generated directly by the production and sale of specific goods. These are known as .... costs. They include materials, factory labour and postage and packing. All other costs, including the cost of running the head office, are .... The latter are mainly fixed costs, in other words they do not change as output/sales change. They include salaries, interest charges and rent/components (delete one).

Firms also look at their average costs, in other words total costs divided by .... This is important because in the long-run a firm must keep average costs below its selling price, or else it will suffer sustained losses.

B Identify the following definitions

1 Costs that change in direct proportion to changes in output. ....

2 All a firm's fixed costs plus its unit variable costs multiplied by output.

   ....

3 Costs that cannot be attributed to a product or a cost centre. ....

C Sketch and label

On the left-hand graph show:

1 Fixed costs of £900.

2 Total costs, if fixed costs are £900 and variable costs are £4 per unit.

On the right-hand graph show:

3 Average fixed costs, using the same figures as in C2.

4 Average total costs, using the same figures as in C2.

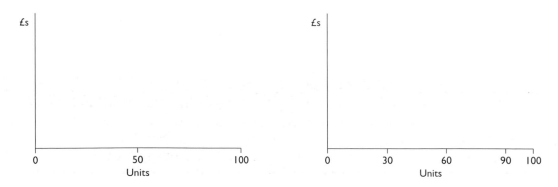

D Anagrams

1 Always a financial burden   SOX FITS DEC   ....

2 Also known as direct   VAST BRAILE SOC   ....

3 Also known as indirect; look up! O, SHE RAVED!   ....

E Calculations

1 During the summer weeks, Devon Ice Creams has fixed overheads of £800 and sales of £4,000. Each ice cream sells for £1 and has direct costs of 25p.

   a) Calculate the total costs for the business in the summer weeks.

   ....

   b) Calculate Devon Ice Cream's average cost per ice cream sold.

   ....

   c) In the winter, the average cost per unit rises. Why?

   ....

2 A firm has £42,000 of fixed costs per month and variable costs of £8 per unit. Current demand is for 1,200 units per month.

   a) Calculate the firm's current average costs per unit.

   ....

   b) Calculate the new average costs, if demand falls to 750 units.

   ....

   c) If the firm's selling price is £65, what is the impact of the demand fall on its profit margin?

   ....

Examiners' **Notes**

Surprisingly, exam students often forget to treat 'total costs' or 'average costs' with suspicion. Remember that they break down into fixed (indirect) and variable (direct). Becoming crystal clear about fixed and variable costs is probably the most important revision starting point. Also look at 'Break-even' and 'Profit'.

Decision trees

A Missing words

Decision trees are diagrams showing the choices and .... events that may occur as a result of a business decision. When drawing the diagram, ... are used to show where a decision is needed and chance events are shown by .... Decision trees encourage the quantification of risk by using a weighted average of the expected outcomes from a decision multiplied by the .... of each outcome occurring. The trees are drawn from .... to right, following a time sequence of what happens when. Calculations are made from .... to left, showing clearly any decisions that have been made.

B Drawing the tree

Which of the following events involve choice and which are governed by chance?

1 The BZQ Co. must decide whether to buy or lease a new machine. ....

2 If it rains on Saturday evening, the funfair's takings will fall by 50%. ....

3 It's 50/50 as to whether the advertising campaign succeeds or fails. ....

4 Research proves that 1 in 5 new products succeeds in the marketplace. ....

5 Either we cut costs sharply or we push for a successful new product launch. ....

C Calculations using weighted averages

1 If there's a 40% chance of selling 2,000 tonnes of apples and a 60% chance of selling 3,000, what's the weighted average outcome? ....

2 A business buying a new robotic machine estimates that there's a 0.1 chance of running costs being £10,000 per year, a 0.6 chance of £30,000 and a 0.3 chance of £50,000. Calculate the weighted average cost outcome. ....

D Answer questions on the tree (shown on the facing page)

1 Calculate the weighted averages at nodes 1 and 2.

....

2 Calculate the net expected value for Launch A and Launch B.

....

3 Explain why the firm might not launch A, even though it has the better net expected value.

....

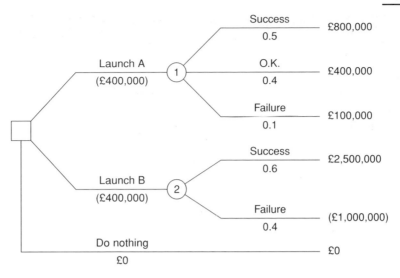

E *Draw the decision tree for the following*

The Denby Bakery must replace its oven. A programmable electric oven from Germany will cost £100,000 and could generate a maximum contribution of £500,000. The chance of this happening is only one in ten. It is five times more likely that the contribution will be £200,000. It is also possible that disappointing demand will place a ceiling of £80,000 on the contribution generated. A gas oven from Yorkshire will cost only £40,000 and is believed to have a 50/50 chance of generating either £150,000 or £80,000 contribution.

a) Draw the tree.

b) Show your calculations, workings and decision.

Delegation and consultation

A Missing words

.... means discussing things with others, then making a decision yourself. .... means passing a................................. (power) down the hierarchy to give staff the scope to make decisions for themselves. Strangely, many students regard consultation as the more democratic of the two approaches. They see delegation as 'giving staff tasks'. Examiners appreciate candidates who can see delegation as a democratic, empowering process. Nevertheless, some managers claim to consult or delegate when in fact they make all the key d................................. and keep all the key tasks for themselves.

B Delegation, Consultation, Empowerment or None of them?

Write D, C, E, or N by each of the following statements.

1 The Head gives the Business Studies department a £1,200 budget for spending on books.

2 At the monthly meeting the Asda store manager asks staff their views on moving to 24-hour opening.

3 The government minister asks his secretary to book a table for lunch.

4 A construction manager asks his deputy to 'look after the new business section from now on'.

5 The Head calls a staff meeting to discuss student discipline and how to improve it.

C Explain why

1 Delegation is an appropriate management technique for a democratic leader.

....

2 Consultation is appropriate for a paternalistic leader.

....

....

3 An authoritarian leader would use neither.

....

Examiners' Notes

Exam students are fine on consultation, but misunderstand delegation. Remember that delegation is a democratic approach – passing power down the hierarchy.

Depreciation

A Missing words

Depreciation spreads the cost of a fixed asset over its expected useful
.... Therefore, if British Airways buys a new plane this year for
£80 million and anticipates using it for the next ten years, it can charge
£............. million per year for ten years instead of £80 million to this year's accounts.
In this way depreciation supports investment by preventing Profit and ....
Accounts from being hit too hard in the short term when fixed assets are bought.

The most common form of depreciation is .... line. This is calculated
using the formula:

....

B Calculations

1   A company buys a BMW for £25,000, anticipating that it will have a useful life
     of three years. At the end of the period its residual value is expected to be
     £7,000.

On the basis of straight-line depreciation, calculate:

a) The first year's depreciation.

....

b) The book value (balance sheet value) of the BMW after two years.

....

2 A firm buys a machine for £130,000. It expects it to have five years of useful life and a
   residual value of £10,000. The firm forecasts gross profits of £40,000 p.a. over the next
   five years.

   a) If the firm depreciates on a straight-line basis, calculate the:

   i)   annual depreciation ....

   ii) accumulated depreciation after three years ....

   iii) book value of the machine after two years ....

   b) If, at the end of year three, the management decides the machine is obsolete and
   must be replaced, what will be the company's year three net profit? ....

   ....

   ....

Economic growth

A Missing words

Economic growth is the rate at which output and spending rises over time.
The usual measurement is the annual percentage change in the GDP (G...........................
D................................ P...) in real terms. The underlying growth rate
in GDP is largely dependent upon improvements in ....
(efficiency) perhaps due to more, or better, investment or an increasingly skilled and
productive workforce.

B Data analysis (1)

Year	Gross Domestic Product at market (money) prices	Gross Domestic Product at real (1995) prices	Index of real GDP 1995 = 100
1995	£714 billion	£714 billion	100.0
1996	£756 billion	£731 billion	102.6
1997	£805 billion	£758 billion	106.2
1998	£852 billion	£778 billion	109.0
1999	£891 billion	£795 billion	111.3
2000	£935 billion	£820 billion	114.9

1 In 2000, the UK population was 60 million. Calculate the money GDP per head data
for that year.

....

2 In the US the equivalent figure was £20,000. Outline three possible reasons for
America's higher figure.

....

....

C True or false?

Place a T or an F by each of the following statements.

1 Since 1990, Japan's rate of economic growth has been much faster than
Britain's.

2 If the rate of economic growth increased, problems of traffic congestion
and pollution would worsen.

3 The rate of economic growth is the main determinant of progress in people's standard of living. ☐

D Data analysis (2)

Examine the graph, then answer the questions below.

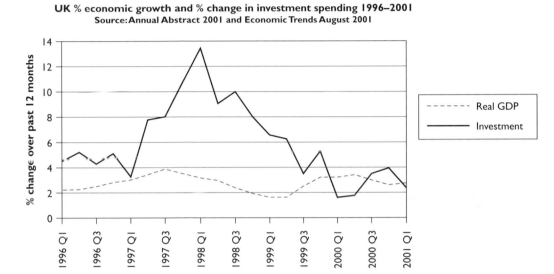

UK % economic growth and % change in investment spending 1996–2001
Source: Annual Abstract 2001 and Economic Trends August 2001

1 For the last 100 years, the rate of economic growth has been about 2.25% in real terms.

   a) How did the period 1996–2001 compare?

   ....

   b) What is meant by 'in real terms'?

   ....

2 It appears that % changes in company investment are more erratic than % change in the economy as a whole. Why might that be?

   ....

   ....

   ....

3 If a car manufacturing firm saw the rate of economic growth dipping towards 0%, how might it respond?

   ....

   ....

   ....

Economies and diseconomies of scale

A Missing words

Economies of scale are factors that cause average .... to fall as a consequence of operating at a .... scale of output.

It is often assumed that they always provide benefits to large firms in every industry. Experience suggests this is not the case. The car industry certainly benefits from technical economies stemming from up-to-date, expensive machinery and purchasing economies such as .... Service businesses such as advertising agencies may find no economies of scale at all.

B Tick the relevant category for each of these factors

Factor	Economy of scale	Diseconomy of scale	Neither
1 Costs arising from poor communication			
2 Effect on the interest rate of borrowing large sums			
3 Impact of automation on labour costs			
4 Rising wages due to shortage of IT staff			
5 Effect on variable costs of bulk buying			
6 Impact of poor staff coordination			

C Distinguish between

1 Buying in bulk *and* Buying materials at the lowest cost

....

....

....

2 Division of labour   *and*   Multi-skilling

....

....

....

3 Economies of scale   *and*   Higher capacity utilisation

....

....

....

D Analysing data

Look at these figures for three chocolate manufacturers then answer the questions below.

	Cardews	Planets	Nestee
Tonnes of chocolate produced per annum	20,000	35,000	10,000
Factory workforce	4,000	5,000	2,500
Product waste/reject %	2.2	2.9	0.9
Cost per tonne of cocoa purchased	£815	£809	£820
Interest charges on bank loans %	6.75	6.25	7.00
Labour turnover %	8	11	10

1 Calculate the productivity level for each chocolate producer (output per worker).

....

....

....

2 Identify and briefly explain two factors that suggest economies of scale.

....

....

....

3 Identify one factor that clearly suggests diseconomies of scale. Briefly explain your answer.

....

....

....

....

Elasticity of demand

A Missing words

1 The demand for price .... goods changes little when prices change.

2 Higher real incomes cut demand for .... goods.

3 Products with low product differentiation have .... price elasticity.

4 Heavy advertising spending is likely to reduce the .... elasticity of demand.

B Anagrams

1 Insensitive to change in a variable   NICE TAILS ....

2 A key determinant of a product's price elasticity   I NOT TIME, COP...............................

3 Price elasticity is always this, income elasticity sometimes   GIVE TENA ....

C Calculations

1 If a 10p price rise on a £2 product cuts demand by 20%, what is its price elasticity?

....

2 A firm selling garden chairs believes their advertising elasticity is about 0.5. Current sales are 2,000 units at £50 each. What is the new sales revenue if advertising spending is doubled?

....

D Identify the following definitions

1 A product where sales change by a larger % than the % price change.

....

2 A product for which sales change little when real incomes change.

....

3 Measurement of the responsiveness of demand to changes in advertising spending.

....

E *What is the effect upon total revenue of the following changes?*

1 A price increase on a price elastic product.

....

2 A price increase on a price inelastic product.

....

3 A price cut on a product with a price elasticity of 1.

....

F *Estimate the elasticities of demand for each of the following*

	Rolls Royce cars	BP petrol	YSL shirts
Price elasticity			
Advertising elasticity			
Income elasticity			

Examiners' Notes

Students tend to merge the elasticities, writing about 'elastic products'. Good analysis relies on separating price elasticity from income (or any other) elasticity. Each has separate causes and consequences; no brand is 'elastic' or 'inelastic'.

Employer–employee relations

A Odd one out

Circle the odd one out in each row. What is the collective term for the other three?

1 Go-slow   Overtime ban   Kanban   Strike

   Collective term: ....

2 Conciliation   Delegation   Arbitration   Mediation

   Collective term: ....

3 Teamworking   Autonomous work group   Quality circle   Job rotation

   Collective term: ....

B Which term is defined by each of the following statements?

1 An organisation founded to promote and
protect the interests of employees. ....

2 Work that is undertaken by staff employed
by a different firm – often on a temporary basis. ....

3 Formal, regular meetings between representatives
of management and shopfloor staff. ....

C Distinguish between

1 Individual bargaining *and* Collective bargaining ....

   ....

   ....

2 Autonomous work groups *and* Teams ....

   ....

   ....

3 Conciliation *and* Arbitration..

   ....

   ....

Employment law

A Missing words

Past evidence suggests that unless .... passes laws to regulate employment practices, discrimination and other unfair practices are likely to be common.

Up until the 1970s, men and women doing identical jobs could be (and were) paid different .... levels. That was made unlawful by the 1970 Equal Pay Act. Open .... discrimination in recruitment or promotion was also legal until the 1968 Race Relations Act.

Despite the potential benefits of these laws, they are criticised by some for being ineffective and by others for interfering in the right of managers to run their business as they see fit.

B Which five terms are defined by the following statements?

1 European legislation that limits the number of hours an employee should work to 48 per week. ....

2 The law that ensures that pay differences are based on skill or experience, not race or gender. ....

3 Showing a preference for one type of person at the expense of another. ....

4 Giving fathers of new-born children the right to time off work. ....

5 Sacking a member of staff for a reason that the law does not consider fair. ....

C Briefly explain

1 A key argument *against* legal intervention to protect employees.

....
....

2 A key argument *in favour* of employment law being the same throughout Europe.

....
....
....

3 A key argument to persuade firms that equal, fair treatment of staff is in their interests.

....

....

D Which law?

Draw arrows to match the legal issue to the relevant law.

I Health and Safety at Work Act 1974	**a)** It is unlawful to recruit staff using criteria that are biased in favour of men rather than women (though some exceptions are allowed)
2 Employment Relations Act 1999	**b)** Employers must provide a safe working environment 'as far as is reasonably practicable'
3 Sex Discrimination Act 1975	**c)** Firms must not show preference on the basis of racial or ethnic factors when selecting staff to go on training courses
4 Race Relations Act 1968	**d)** Over any 13-week period staff should not have to average more than 48 working hours per week
5 Working Time Directive 1999	**e)** Employers must recognise and negotiate with trade unions if more than 50% of the workforce are members or vote to become so

E Anagrams

1 Remuneration that's fair to all   PLAQUE, YA? ....

2 Where to take a case for unfair dismissal   LO, TINY BRUTE LAMP MEN

....

3 A repeated action can cause strain or injury   TIE RIPE VET ....

Examiners' Notes

You need not revise any law in detail, but it is useful to have a general understanding of health and safety, employment protection and regulations about the minimum wage and the Working Time Directive.

European Union

A Missing words

> The European Union comprises 15 member states, all of which must adhere to certain rules connected with trade and the law. All EU countries undertake to have completely free trade between member states. Therefore there can be no .... (import taxes), no .... (physical limits on the number of imports) and no non-tariff barriers.
>
> The EU began in 1957 as the Common Market, and was later called the EEC, then the EC until, in 1993, the name European Union was established.
>
> Over the coming years, a key issue for the union will be whether to allow in former communist countries from central and eastern Europe such as Hungary and Poland. Because wage rates are about one quarter of those in west Europe, there is a fear that these countries will prove too competitive for many traditional British industries, such as textiles and shipbuilding.

B True or false?

Place a T or an F by each of the following statements.

1 An unemployed British bricklayer is free to get a job in any EU country. ☐

2 Goods coming into the European Union are charged import taxes – usually at a rate of 10%. ☐

3 The EU provides UK firms with a 'home market' of 375 million people. ☐

4 Joining the Euro will add to the costs of importing and exporting within Europe. ☐

5 EU legislation has improved fairness at work for part-time workers and women. ☐

C Strengths and weaknesses

For each example of EU practice, give the letters of one advantage and one disadvantage from the list below.

1 Free movement of labour between EU countries. ....

2 Social Chapter to improve protection of staff rights at work. ....

3 Single market legislation to eliminate barriers to free trade. ....

4 European Single Currency (the Euro). ....

Advantage	Disadvantage
a) Increased competition forces more efficiency and lower prices	**w)** If too costly, may make EU labour uncompetitive with non-EU
b) Reduces supply bottlenecks if staff can be hired from overseas	**x)** Individual countries cannot set interest rates to suit themselves
c) Lowers the risks and costs of exporting (within EU)	**y)** Removing barriers Europe-wide stops countries making own rules
d) Cuts risk that firms compete on cost by lowering safety standards	**z)** A potential weakness if people only speak their own language

D Big EU issues

1 Should Britain withdraw from the EU? Give two reasons for, and two against, withdrawal.

Reasons to withdraw..

....

Reasons to stay in ....

....

2 Should Britain join the Euro? Give two reasons for and two reasons against joining.

Reasons to join Euro ....

....

Reasons not to join Euro ....

....

Exchange rates

A Missing words

> The exchange rate links currencies together by showing a price at which they can be bought and sold.
>
> If the £ falls in value, it can buy less of any foreign currency. For example, if the £ equalled $1.50, but then the £ fell by 10%, every £ could then buy .... This would mean .... £s would be needed to buy any US $ product. Therefore, imports from America would become more expensive. This would .... the volume of imports. Although a falling £ makes imports more expensive, it benefits our exporters as they are able to sell overseas more cheaply.

B Briefly explain

1 Why firms selling price elastic exports suffer most from a high pound.

....

....

2 Why a government wanting to reduce inflation would want a high £.

....

....

3 Why a high pound hits the profit margins of UK exporters.

....

....

4 Why most exporting firms want Britain to join the Euro.

....

....

C Calculate

1 The Leyland Type 17 Truck sells in the UK for £32,000.

a) When there were 3DM to the £, how much should it have been sold for in Germany?

....

....

b) If the £ fell by 10% against the Deutschmark, what price would then be charged for the Type 17 in Germany?

....

....

2 a) Calculate the correct US $ price to charge for a UK-produced squidget, given that:

> Labour productivity = 5 squidgets per hour
>
> Wage rate = £6
>
> Other variable costs = £2.50 per unit
>
> Pricing is on the basis of 100% mark up
>
> £1 = $1.50

b) Explain why the exporter may actually price the product at $9.99.

....

....

D Fill in the gaps

1 A rise in the £ means our export volumes are likely to ....

2 A fall in the £ is likely to push import prices ....

3 A fall in the £ .... Britain's international competitiveness.

4 Importers such as Dixons love the pound to be ....

5 Joining the Euro would fix the value of the £ against other ....
currencies for ever.

Examiners' **Notes**

Remember: £ up means £ buys more dollars, Euros etc. And when the £ is up, UK international competitiveness falls, i.e. UK exports cost more; foreign imports to the UK cost less.

Financial efficiency

A Missing words

The financial efficiency of a business can be measured by financial ratios such as asset .... , stock .... and .... days (the average time customers take to pay). When these data are compared with previous years or with rival firms it is possible to consider whether the firm is being run well or badly. The information required for this analysis is usually only available for .... companies (plcs) either from their annual report and accounts or from sources such as Sequencer or Companies House.

B Formulae

Fill in the gaps.

1 Asset turnover ratio $\dfrac{\text{Sales revenue}}{\text{..}}$ = Sales generated per £ invested in assets

2 Stock turnover ratio $\dfrac{\text{..}}{\text{Stock (at cost)}}$ = Number of times per year stock is sold and replaced

3 Debtor days ratio $\dfrac{\text{Debtors}}{\text{Average daily ....}}$ = Average time taken by customers to pay bills

C Calculations

1   A firm has annual sales of £730,000, assets employed of £365,000, debtors of £80,000 and creditors of £120,000.

Calculate:

a) the asset turnover ratio ....

b) the debtor days ratio ....

2   Last year, Dart Greengrocers had a stock turnover of 24. This year sales have risen 10% to £920,000, cost of sales are £600,000 and the balance sheet shows stocks of £30,000.

a) Calculate Dart's stock turnover this year. ....

b) Briefly analyse Dart's efficiency of stock management this year.

....

....

....

....

....

D Which ratio shows what?

By each ratio, write down the letter(s) of the possible indicator(s).

Financial efficiency ratio	Indicator
1 Asset turnover	**a)** Could indicate the need for a more expert credit controller
	b) May suggest the need to sell off under-used assets
2 Stock turnover	**c)** May suggest looking into the use of credit factoring
3 Debtor days	**d)** May point to the need for a move to JIT
	e) Could point to a new low-price, high-volume sales strategy

E Explain one risk from each of the following

1 Asset turnover being too high. ....

2 Stock turnover being too low. ....

3 Debtor days being too high. ....

4 Asset turnover being too low. ....

5 Debtor days being cut sharply. ....

Examiners' **Notes**

Remember that financial efficiency comes from good operational efficiency (e.g. stock and quality control), good marketing that adds value and productive, highly motivated staff. 'Finance' should not be treated in isolation.

Fiscal policy

A Missing words

> Governments know that successful management of the economy is the key to re-election. Therefore they focus on a clear strategy for meeting economic .... such as raising economic growth and reducing unemployment.
>
> Fiscal policy is one of the main tools available for implementing economic strategy. It involves planning the level of .... required to provide the finances to fund government spending. Fiscal policy involves every spending decision and every taxation decision made by government. It also includes the overall balance between government income and expenditure, known as the fiscal balance.

B Identify the following definitions, then find the word formed from the first letter of each one

1 A tax that hits the better off harder than the less well off. ....

2 A tax that hits the less well off harder than the better off. ....

3 A tax levied on goods, not incomes. ....

4 Government spending on investment, perhaps in infrastructure such as roads. ....

5 Zones in deprived areas given special tax concessions, to attract employers. ....

   Answer ....

C Draw arrows to match the economic objective to the corresponding fiscal policy

Economic objective	Fiscal policy
1 Improve the skill level in the economy	a) Tax relief on capital expenditure
2 Reduce inflationary pressures	b) Provide grants for firms in Assisted Areas
3 Increase business investment	c) Spend more on advice centres for entrepreneurs
4 Boost new business formation	d) Increase the % rate of income tax
5 Encourage firms to locate away from London	e) Boost government spending on education

Flotation

A Missing words

Public .... companies (plcs) are able to advertise their shares and sell them to any member of the public. The starting point for this is usually to float the shares on the stock exchange; this is known as a company .... The business issues a prospectus that sets out the history, the financial circumstances and the future plans of the business. Investors are then invited to buy .... in the business. If there is lots of demand for the shares, their price .... , making a quick profit for the early investors.

B Give two reasons why

1 A firm's shares might fall below the issue (flotation) price.

   ....

   ....

2 A growing small firm might want to float its shares on the stock market.

   ....

   ....

C True or false?

Place a T or an F by each of the following statements.

1 A firm may float fewer than 50% of its shares in order to ensure its independence. ☐

2 A firm's original investors may only be willing to dilute their shareholdings when they think the growth stage is over. ☐

3 Once on the stock market a firm will not be allowed to windowdress its accounts. ☐

4 Floating on the stock market may cost as much as £500,000 in fees to City advisers. ☐

D State the phrase or term explained by each of the following

1 After flotation the managers of a plc may develop objectives that are quite different from those of the shareholders. This is almost impossible within a private limited company. ....

2 Pressure to achieve high levels of profit within the current financial year may persuade the head of a plc to make decisions that are not in the firm's long-term best interests.

   ....

Gearing

A Missing words

> Gearing assesses a firm's dependence upon .... It is done by
> measuring the firm's long-term loans as a percentage of its ....
> employed. If gearing is 25%, therefore, it means that a quarter of the firm's capital is
> .... A firm is considered to be highly geared if loans are more than
> half the capital employed. High gearing may make it difficult for a firm to meet
> interest payments, especially in a period of poor trading or when ....
> rates rise.

B Cause, effect or neither?

Would each of the following be a *cause* of higher gearing, or an *effect*, or *neither*? Put a C,
an E or an N by each.

1 High overhead costs ....

2 Taking out an additional long-term loan ....

3 Introducing 5% price increases ....

4 The business making a loss after tax ....

5 A threat to survival when loans must be repaid ....

6 Increases variable costs ....

7 Financing a take-over by loan capital ....

8 May help finance rapid growth ....

C True or false?

Place a T or an F by each of the following statements.

1 A firm with zero gearing is implying that it cannot see how to make a higher
rate of return than the cost of borrowing capital (the interest rate). □

2 A firm with 80% gearing is vulnerable because only 20% of its capital employed
is its own money (the rest is borrowed). So one year of bad losses may wipe it
out completely. □

3 A firm with 33% gearing is safe because its rate of return is well above the
cost of capital (the interest rate). □

4 A firm with 80% gearing could cut the level if it could sell off some assets
above book value, then use the cash to repay some loans. □

5   Capital employed consists of loan capital, share capital and reserves (accumulated, retained profit). ☐

D Key questions

1   Can a firm have too low a gearing level?

....

....

2   Why are new, small firms likely to be highly geared?

....

....

....

E Calculations

1   A firm has £400,000 of long-term loans, £100,000 of share capital and £500,000 of reserves. Calculate its gearing level.

....

....

2   A firm has loans £40,000, share capital £10,000, reserves £30,000 and fixed assets of £80,000.

   a) Calculate the gearing level. ....

   b) What would be the new gearing level, if the firm borrowed an extra £20,000?

....

....

3   If a firm with £2 million of capital employed is 70% geared

   a) What is its debt level? ....

   b) If it borrows an extra £1 million, what is its new gearing level?

....

Examiners' Notes

In boom times, commentators and analysts treat low gearing as a sign of corporate weakness; but do not follow fashion; high gearing always adds risk and should only be accepted for a short period of time for a business that is growing rapidly.

Identifying a business opportunity

A Missing words

Many people think that the main constraint on starting a new business is obtaining finance. In fact this is unlikely to be very difficult if an attractive business opportunity has been identified and researched. The need is to find a gap in the market that can be filled in a way that will be hard for others to imitate. A new product invention can be .... , which gives up to twenty years of protection from direct .... James Dyson did this with his innovative Dual Cyclone (bagless) cleaner.

Retail businesses will rarely be based on a new invention that can be patented, but they will be able to register the c............................ on the brand name, logos and packaging they use.

B Place in a logical order

These tasks should be undertaken prior to opening a new retail outlet; but in which order? Use numbers 1 to 6 to give correct order.

a) Advertising the store opening in the local paper ☐

b) Obtaining background census data on the local population size and type ☐

c) Planning the number and type of staff needed ☐

d) Conducting some in-depth interviews with a small sample of consumers ☐

e) Advertising for – and selecting – staff ☐

f) Mapping the area, noting the location and type of competitors ☐

C Data response

Look at the text and diagram (on the facing page), then answer the questions following.

Jimmy Yip was on the phone like a flash when he heard that the only Chinese restaurant in the shopping centre had closed down. His family's restaurant on Don Lane had been struggling ever since the shopping centre had opened five years ago. Now was Jimmy's chance to start his first business.

1   Briefly comment on whether Jimmy is justified in sounding so optimistic.

....

....

Map of Don town centre, showing Chinese restaurants

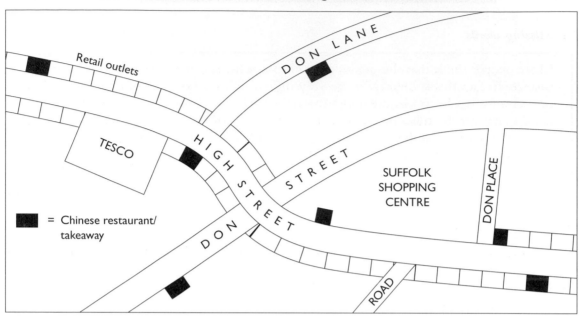

2 Identify two pieces of small budget research Jimmy should carry out before proceeding.

....

....

....

....

3 Businesses such as local restaurants cannot afford heavy advertising. Suggest two ways in which Jimmy might publicise his opening?

....

....

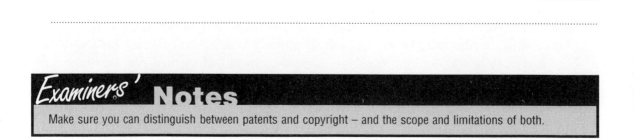

Examiners' **Notes**

Make sure you can distinguish between patents and copyright – and the scope and limitations of both.

Industrial democracy

A Missing words

Industrial democracy means establishing methods by which the views of the majority of staff have an impact upon strategic decisions made within a business. In a minor way, this could be achieved by .... , if only managers would take staff opinions seriously enough to act on them. More realistic is to set up a structure such as .... councils (in which staff representatives from all levels meet regularly with managers), or employee .... (where the option to attend the Annual General Meeting helps make staff views influential).

B Democracy, consultation or lip service?

Put a D (democracy), a C (consultation) or an L (lip service) by each of the following. Briefly explain your reasoning.

1 Hit hard by economic downturn, FD Co. arranges a 2-day discussion session with staff representatives to discuss how best to reduce the wage bill. Full data on salaries, conditions and bonus agreements are provided. ☐

....

2 After a secret board meeting, GJX Co. announces a 7-day consultation exercise on whether a loss-making product should be discontinued. Staff are told to arrange appointments themselves with their boss, or to put views in writing, addressed to the Managing Director. ☐

....

3 The Welding work group has been given a budget of £200,000 to buy new equipment and three days off to visit suppliers before making a choice. ☐

....

C Explain the possible value to a firm of having

1 Employee shareholders. ....

....

2 Works councils. ....

....

3 Autonomous work groups. ....

....

D Suggest two reasons why

1 Successful industrial democracy might boost staff motivation.

....

....

2 Democratic structures such as works councils would not work if senior managers have Theory X attitudes.

....

....

3 Successful industrial democracy might make it hard to cope with a trading downturn.

....

....

E Data response

Beacon Railways had invested £240 million on new trains. The Engineering Director was proud of his purchasing decisions and was angry to overhear a mechanic say, 'We didn't even know it was happening, let alone contribute our ideas'.

Two years later, the new trains were ready to roll, but in the following months derailments rose sharply leading to increased levels of passenger delay. The track engineers were sure that the new trains were too heavy and fast for the old track, but no one was willing to tell the Engineering Director. Then came a terrible crash and a public enquiry.

1 Explain how Beacon Railways might have benefited from a works council.

....

....

....

2 Discuss whether the law should force all large businesses to have a worker representative on the board.

....

....

....

....

Industrial policy

A Missing words

Industrial policy is the government's plan for promoting business success by attempting to match financial, capital and human resources to industry's needs. This might include providing low interest rate loans to new, small businesses, extra spending on the infrastructure such as .... or .... , or the promotion of new training schemes such as Modern Apprenticeships.

Governments do not *have* to have an industrial policy. They may adopt a laissez-faire approach in which government deliberately holds back, allowing the market to allocate resources without government ....

B Draw arrows to match the government policy (on the right) to the objective (on the left)

Government objective	Industrial policy measure
1 Reduce unemployment in Cornwall and Co. Durham	**a)** Offer support and subsidies to companies considering whether to locate a factory in Britain or elsewhere
2 Boost the number of high-tech business start-ups	**b)** Establish Learning and Skills Councils to meet local training needs
3 Reduce the failure rate of new business start-ups	**c)** Tax relief on R&D spending by small firms
4 Maintain a high level of inward investment	**d)** Provide capital to support major long-term investments such as developing the Super-Jumbo jet
5 Reduce the skills shortages that constrain growth	**e)** Building new motorway and high-speed rail links
6 Increase Britain's long run growth rate	**f)** Establish a Small Firms Service to provide advice and training for entrepreneurs

C Briefly explain the relevance of these concepts to industrial policy

1 Opportunity cost. ....
....

2 Laissez-faire beliefs.
....
....

3 Regional economic imbalances.
....
....

Inflation

A Missing words

Inflation is the rate of rise in the average .... level. It is usually measured over a .... month period making it easy to compare with other annual measures such as interest rates and the rate of rise in average earnings.

In the UK the main measure of inflation is the RPI (the ....). The causes of inflation can be split into two types: .... –push and .... –pull.

B Sort the cause

The following are causes of inflation. Sort them into **(1)** cost-push and **(2)** demand-pull.

a) fall in the value of the £

b) rapidly rising consumer spending

c) shortage of production capacity

d) world shortage of key commodities such as oil

e) rising wage expectations

f) large increase in government spending

1 Cost-push inflation. ....

....

....

2 Demand-pull inflation. ....

....

....

C Effects of inflation

1 What are the effects of high inflation upon businesses? Two are listed below; outline two others.

> High inflation focuses the mind of the consumer upon price; this can undermine the power and value added of brand names.
>
> But inflation helps firms with high borrowings. Inflation reduces the value of money, so a £100,000 loan that seems impossible to repay today may seem quite affordable in 10 years' time.

a) ....

....

b) ....

....

D Fill in the gaps

1 a) When there is deflation, it means prices are going ....

b) If inflation is 3% while average earnings are rising by 5%, real incomes are going .... by ....%.

c) Tradex Paint is priced on a cost-push basis; its current price is £9.75. Inflationary pressures will soon require a 4% price rise. This will push the price up to .... , which breaks through what may be an important .... price barrier.

d) Inflationary expectations are crucial, because if people .... prices to rise, they will try to push for higher .... to ensure that their real earnings remain constant.

Examiners' Notes

Inflation is one of the most poorly analysed concepts in business studies; do *not* say = prices up, therefore demand falls (and recession results); *do* say = prices up and wages up, therefore money loses its value but demand for goods stays pretty constant.

IT (information technology)

A Missing words

Information technology is the processing and communication of data by and between people and .... It has had an increasingly major impact upon business since the 1970s.

IT increases the speed of many operations, such as data collection, analysis and distribution. This allows new ways of working, such as .... (working from home, connected to the office electronically). It also helps accountants establish an effective system of .... and variance analysis.

B Follow the format in 1 below to explain how a firm could use IT to help deal with its stakeholders

1 **Suppliers:** intranet links enable suppliers to check your sales and stock levels, and therefore anticipate your order levels.

2 **Business customers:** ....

....

3 **Local pressure groups:** ....

....

4 **Staff:** ....

....

C Which type of information technology is defined as follows

1 Stores information that can then be used flexibly, e.g. finding all customers in the Leeds area. ....

2 Links design drawings done on computer to computer-controlled production systems. ....

3 Used in shops to record the precise details of the products bought by customers. ....

4 Links computers world-wide via the telephone, allowing e-mails and searching for data. ....

D Data response

Look at the data below and then answer the questions.

	Company A	Company B	Company C
% of turnover spent on IT systems	4.5	6.75	2.3
Lead time: time between customer order and delivery	4.5 weeks	1.5 weeks	3.5 weeks
% of staff working from home	3	12	1
Time to produce accounts after end of financial year	11 weeks	5 weeks	14 weeks
Stock turnover ratio	4.2 times	5.0 times	4.5 times

1 Identify three pieces of evidence that justify Company B's heavy IT spending.

....

....

2 Give two possible reasons why Company C achieves a faster lead time than Company A. ....

....

3 State two ways in which IT investment could help increase stock turnover.

....

....

4 Identify two possible benefits from having accounting information more speedily.

....

....

E Give two reasons why

1 A firm's competitiveness may be damaged by poor IT systems.

....

2 Internal communication may be damaged by excessive use of IT, e.g. e-mail.

....

....

3 Heavy investment in IT is not enough to make a firm a world-beater.

....

....

Interest rates

A Missing words

Interest rates are the price of .... , measured as an annual percentage payment. Therefore the rate of interest (the price) is determined by the supply and .... for money.

If consumers and businesses feel optimistic about their future, they may want to borrow money to buy assets such as houses or factories. This demand for borrowed money may push up the price, i.e. the interest rate. If interest rates .... , the consumers may become reluctant to buy goods on credit; therefore consumer spending may ....

B Which of the following are likely effects of a sharp rise in interest rates? Tick the relevant ones

a) Higher mortgage payments may hit spending by young families. ☐

b) The value of the £ may rise on the foreign exchange market. ☐

c) Consumers may cut back spending on luxuries. ☐

d) Firms may cut investment spending, as finance is too costly. ☐

e) Firms may increase their demand for borrowed money. ☐

f) Spending on consumer durables may fall, e.g. cars and houses. ☐

g) Consumers may cut back spending on necessities. ☐

h) Inflation may increase due to demand–pull pressures. ☐

i) Consumer and business confidence may be hit. ☐

C Calculations

1   A firm's operating profits are steady at £800,000 a year. To calculate its pre-tax profit, interest payments must be deducted. It has a £4 million variable-rate loan. Interest rates rise from 6% to 10%.

Calculate the effect upon the firm's pre-tax profit.

....

....

2 House prices are sensitive to changes in the interest (and therefore mortgage) rate. For every 1% rise in interest rates, house prices tend to fall by 2.5%.

Calculate the impact upon the price of a £200,000 house of a 3% rise in interest rates.

....

....

D Explain in your own words

1 Why the value of the £ is likely to increase if UK interest rates rise.

....

....

....

2 Why rising interest rates may reduce the number of business start-ups.

....

....

....

....

3 Why firms cut their stock levels when interest rates rise.

....

....

....

....

E True or false?

Place a T or an F by each of the following statements.

1 Small firms are hit hardest by rising interest rates, because they are often financed by overdrafts. ☐

2 A fall in interest rates particularly benefits producers of durable goods and luxuries. ☐

3 A fall in interest rates makes firms less keen to borrow money. ☐

4 A sharp rise in interest rates may lead to a recession and therefore reduce demand-pull inflationary pressures. ☐

International competitiveness

A Missing words

International competitiveness measures the ability of the businesses within a country to compete with those from overseas. Competitiveness depends upon price and non-price factors. The former depend largely upon production and other costs plus the exchange rate.

If the £ is .... it will be difficult for UK-based firms to compete. Non-price factors include the quality of the design, the quality of production, service and after-sales .... plus the cleverness of the branding and marketing. Mercedes cars are highly competitive internationally, even though they are premium priced. For Ford, low costs are essential to enable the product to charge a competitive ....

B Briefly explain how each of the following could affect the competitiveness of Nissan UK

1 Heavy spending on Research & Development.

....

....

....

2 A 9% increase in workforce productivity.

....

....

....

3 A switch from mass to batch production.

....

....

....

4 A 10% fall in the value of the £ against the Euro.

....

....

....

C Data response

Look at this data then answer the questions that follow.

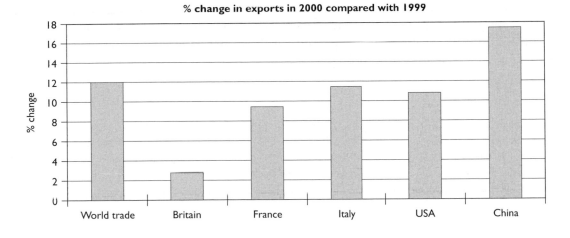

% change in exports in 2000 compared with 1999

1 Why might a developing country such as China be able to expand export sales so effectively?

....

....

2 Identify two factors that might explain Britain's relatively weak export performance in 2000.

....

....

D Helping yourself to cut costs

1 Identify two fixed costs that could be cut without a direct effect on sales.

a) ....   b) ....

2 Identify two ways to cut the cost of raw materials used.

a) ....   b) ....

3 Identify two costs that might be cut following a merger with a rival firm.

a) ....

b) ....

Investment appraisal

A Missing words

Capital investment appraisal is carried out by forecasting the .... flows involved in capital projects. As this process involves forecasting many years into the future, it is subject to a great deal of ....

There are three main methods of .... appraisal: .... period calculates how long it will take for the firm to recoup its initial investment outlay; .... rate of .... measures average annual profit as a percentage of the sum invested and net .... (NPV) discounts future cash flows to calculate their present day value. As long as the NPV on an investment exceeds £ .... it is worth pursuing.

B Net annual cash flows on an investment are forecast to be

	£000
NOW	(600)
End of year 1	100
End of year 2	400
End of year 3	400
End of year 4	180

Calculate

a) The pay-back period.

....

....

b) Average rate of return.

....

....

C Data response

The board of Burford Ltd is meeting to decide whether to invest £500,000 in an automated packing machine or into a new customer service centre. The production manager has estimated the cash flows from the two investments to calculate the following table

	Packing machine	Service centre
Pay-back	1.75 years	3.5 years
NPV	+£28,500	+£25,600

1 On purely quantitative grounds, which would you choose and why?

....

....

....

....

....

2 Identify four other factors the board should consider before making a final decision?

a) ....

b) ....

c) ....

d) ....

D *The cash flows on two alternative projects are estimated to be*

	Project A			Project B	
	Cash in	Cash out		Cash in	Cash out
Year 0	–	£50,000		–	£50,000
Year 1	£60,000	£30,000		£10,000	£10,000
Year 2	£80,000	£40,000		£40,000	£20,000
Year 3	£40,000	£24,000		£60,000	£30,000
Year 4	£20,000	£20,000		£84,000	£40,000

Discount factors (at 8%) are: Year 1 0.93, Year 2 0.86, Year 3 0.79, Year 4 0.735. Carry out a full investment appraisal to decide which (if either) of the projects should be undertaken. Interest rates are currently 8%.

....

....

....

....

....

....

....

....

....

....

Just In Time

A Missing words

Just In Time is a method of operating with minimal stocks in which deliveries arrive just in time to allow production to continue. So, instead of having a b............................ stock available just in case it is needed, a JIT system must be planned so carefully that mistakes do not lead to expensive disruptions to production.

JIT needs to be thought of as a production philosophy rather than just a method of stock c............................ . This is because it has huge implications for quality control, supplier relationships and links with customers (so that changes in demand can be anticipated).

B Match the characteristic to the method

Complete the following, matching the characteristics from the list below to each method of operation.

1 Just In Time ....   2 Just In Case ....

a) Several suppliers per item required, to maximise competition

b) Total reliance on delivery reliability of suppliers

c) Plenty of scope for purchasing economies of scale

d) Need to keep suppliers fully informed, so they can anticipate demand

e) Suppliers need superb quality management, so that deliveries are near-perfect

C For each of the following, outline two reasons why

1 A firm's finances may benefit from a move to JIT.

....

....

2 A firm with poor staff morale may struggle to introduce JIT successfully.

....

....

3 A firm's marketing strategy may be affected by a move to JIT.

....

....

D Data response

Three months ago, Dart Co.'s dynamic new Chief Executive switched to a JIT stock control and production system. Look at this week's benchmark data below, then answer the questions.

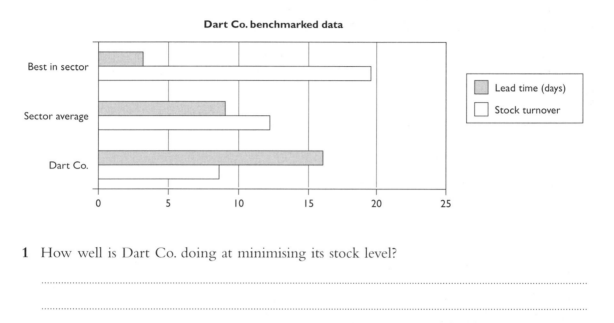

Dart Co. benchmarked data

1 How well is Dart Co. doing at minimising its stock level?

....

....

2 Why might the move to JIT have worsened customer lead times?

....

....

Examiners' **Notes**

Make sure you explain Just In Time as a production strategy, not just a stock policy. For manufacturers, a JIT approach requires superb communications with customers and suppliers and a highly flexible production system.

Kaizen

A Missing words

> Kaizen means taking a series of regular small steps forward that lead to .... improvement.
>
> This Japanese approach is the opposite of F.W. ....'s method of bringing in consultants who recommend wholesale changes to working methods. The value of kaizen is that it emphasises *continuous*, i.e. that methods of working can always be improved and therefore there is no ultimate 'best' way. This opens up influence in the workplace to ordinary staff, any of whom might have a bright idea for a small change that improves performance. Successful use of kaizen relies on well-motivated staff.

B Major mistakes

The following firms attempted radical change that backfired. For each firm, suggest two possible reasons for the failure of their new strategy:

1 In 2000, Marks & Spencer dropped several of their traditional suppliers and switched to buying more cheaply from overseas.

....

....

2 In 1999/2000, Iceland Foods attempted to move from selling mass market goods on price, to only selling organic foods.

....

....

3 In the late 1990s, BMW – then owners of Rover Cars – invested heavily in automated production lines at its UK factories.

....

....

C Give two reasons

1 Why staff morale may be helped by kaizen rather than radical change.

....

....

2 Why a kaizen group meeting weekly may help to boost productivity.

....

....

3 Why regular improvements to productivity are especially important in highly
   competitive markets.

....

....

....

....

D Data response

Two years ago Page Electronics plc started a weekly kaizen meeting between
shopfloor staff, R&D and the engineering staff. Look at the following data from
Page, then answer the questions below.

	Output per worker	Defects per 100 units	% of deliveries on time
2 years ago	124 units per week	7.5	61.5
1 year ago	126 units per week	7.6	63.8
Now	139 units per week	6.9	70.6

1 Suggest two ways in which kaizen group meetings might help to reduce product defect
   levels.

....

....

2 Why may it have taken a year before significant improvements started to show through?

....

....

3 In the coming year, the kaizen group has decided to focus mainly on deliveries rather
   than productivity. Why might it have chosen to do this?

....

....

Leadership

A Missing words

According to management guru Warren Bennis, leadership is 'the capacity to create a compelling vision and translate it into action and sustain it'. Inspiring staff towards a common purpose can be achieved by clever leaders, no matter what leadership style they employ. Some leaders show charisma, such as Richard Branson, while others lead by example, such as Manchester United's Roy Keane.

.... leaders may give orders while .... ones empower their staff, but either style can be effective if the aims are sufficiently clear and appealing.

B Distinguish between a manager (M) and a leader (L)

Put an M or an L against the following statements.

1 Creates and implements effective systems of work. ☐

2 Prioritises well, by selecting the key tasks. ☐

3 Organises events efficiently. ☐

4 Has innovative new ideas, and puts them into action. ☐

5 Can visualise the next step for the business. ☐

6 Gains great satisfaction from meeting budgets. ☐

7 Enjoys planning a major deal, such as a takeover. ☐

8 When faced with a choice, judges the best option. ☐

9 Excellent at running a department. ☐

10 Can inspire people to give of their best. ☐

C Leadership styles (1)

Fill in the blanks.

1 An .... leader keeps information and decision making at the top.

2 A leader who thinks of staff as members of his/her family can be called

....

3 A .... leader discusses then sets clear objectives, then delegates the power to meet them.

D Leadership styles (2)

Write down the letters of two characteristics that apply to each of the following leadership styles.

1 Authoritarian ....   2 Democratic ....

3 Laissez-faire ....   4 Paternalistic ....

---

a) Social needs fully catered for

b) Staff lack clear direction

c) Delegation within clear goals

d) Physical and safety needs catered for

e) Criticism or argument may be harshly dealt with

f) Staff who can cope with pressure may feel hugely empowered

g) Decision making will be rapid

h) Able staff will enjoy the involvement in decision making

E Explain briefly what is meant by the following sayings about leadership

1 'Managers do things right. Leaders do the right thing.' (Warren Bennis)

....

....

2 'A leader is a dealer in hope.' (Napoleon Bonaparte)

....

....

3 'When a great leader's work is done, the people say "We did it ourselves".' (Lao-Tzu)

....

....

Examiners' Notes

The style of leadership within a workplace culture is all-important, but just how important is the leader him or herself? Is s/he worth earnings measured in £millions per year? Probably yes, given the damage a poor leader can inflict on a firm and its staff.

Lean production

A Missing words

Lean producers focus on minimising .... in the use of resources such as materials, labour and time. This applies in the factory, where .... supply systems are used to minimise stock levels and 'right first time' production improves .... It also applies to product development teams, who use simultaneous engineering to ensure that new products are brought to the market as quickly as possible.

B Circle the odd one out

1 Division of labour	Cell	Team
2 Flow	Bodge	Job
3 Kanban	Kaizen	Kaibosh
4 Just In Time	Just In Case	Zero buffer stock
5 Fault free supplies	Reliable suppliers	High work-in-progress

C Identify the following definitions, then find the word formed from the first letter of each one

1 Desired minimum stock level. ....

2 The cost of missing out on the next best alternative. ....

3 The volume of finished product coming from a production system. ....

4 The collective term for raw materials, work-in-progress and finished goods. ....

5 A crucial resource that can be wasted if it is not watched. ....

Answer ....

D Anagrams

1 A continuous process of small steps forward

TO VERMIN PEM

....

2 Dividing a flow system into units/teams

NO DTI CULL, CORP E

....

3 Each worker responsible for own quality

SIGH NECK FELC

....

E Fill in the gaps

1 Job, ... and flow are the three main ways of producing. Lean production attempts to get the best aspects of each.

2 Keeping output constant at a time when labour usage is falling causes a rise in

....

3 Under-utilising capacity causes unnecessarily high .... or .... costs per unit.

4 .... engineering encourages design and development work to happen at the same time.

F Which is the lean producer?

State which of the two producers, A or B, is the lean producer and briefly explain why.

	Producer A	Producer B
Days of materials stock held	2.5	14.5
% quality reject rate found by quality inspectors	1.2	7.2
Average output per hour	115.2	127.9

....

....

....

....

....

Examiners' Notes

Beware of making lean production seem like nice/good/sensible production, i.e. a woolly mush of good things. Lean production means JIT, high quality/low waste and responding flexibly to customer orders; but this is expensive, so unsuited to mass production of standard items such as Mars Bars.

Liquidity

A Missing words

Liquidity measures the ability of a firm to find the .... to pay its bills.

A highly liquid business has plenty of cash, so even if a customer fails to pay on time, there is still sufficient cash for the firm to keep paying its own .... A firm with poor liquidity may struggle to pay its suppliers and may even be unable to pay staff their wages. A big order may embarrass a business with .... liquidity, because it cannot find the cash to buy the materials it needs.

A firm's liquidity can be tested on its balance sheet through the acid .... ratio. Accountants recommend that the ratio should be about 1:1, i.e. £1 of cash + debtors for every £1 of current liabilities.

B Effects on liquidity

Tick to show whether the following events would make a firm's short-term liquidity go up or down or would have no effect.

	Liquidity up	Liquidity down	No effect
1 A debtor pays earlier than expected			
2 The firm repays a long-term loan			
3 Seasonal stockbuilding before Christmas			
4 A fixed asset sold for cash			
5 The firm invests heavily in R&D			
6 A new fixed asset financed by a long-term loan			

C Give two

1 Problems caused by low liquidity.

....

2 Ways to solve a short–term liquidity crisis.

....

....

3 Ways to rebuild liquidity in the medium term.

....

D State one possible cause and one possible effect of each of the following

1 A toy firm has an acid test ratio of 0.25.

Cause ....

Effect ....

2 A brewery has an acid test ratio of 3.4.

Cause ....

Effect ....

3 A supermarket chain has negative working capital.

Cause ....

Effect ....

E Poor liquidity

On the left are listed four situations where liquidity is likely to be poor. Draw arrows to match each with one of the explanations given on the right.

1 Starting up a new small business	a) Operating below break-even eats away at liquidity
2 Where the job takes a long time to complete	b) Too little power to force the customer to pay on time
3 A small firm supplying a large one	c) Suppliers will not give credit, yet customers expect it
4 A seaside hotel in the winter	d) A long gap between cash out and cash in

F Analyse how a firm's liquidity can be poor even if it is operating profitably

....

....

Location of business

A Missing words

With more than 70% of the British economy supplying services, business location decisions are rarely about manufacturing these days. Hotels, restaurants and shops know that location is crucial to sales success. Top locations such as London's Oxford Street are very expensive, but may be worth every penny.

In manufacturing, it may still be important to know whether the product is .... –increasing or .... –reducing. Even in the s................................ (manufacturing) sector, though, qualitative factors are often more important, such as whether there are nice places to live locally.

B True or false?

Place a T or an F by each of the following statements.

1 Multinational manufacturing companies invest most of their funds in plants in developing countries where wage rates are very low. □

2 Government funds and grants are a trivial part of most investment decisions. □

3 Selling over the internet makes a firm's physical location much less important. □

4 Japanese and Korean firms locate in Europe to avoid the tariffs placed on trade into the EU. □

C Which location features match which business?

For each of the businesses listed below, write down the letters corresponding to ideal location features.

1 A local independent chemists shop. ....

2 A Coca-Cola bottling plant. ....

3 A new Japanese micro–electronics factory. ....

4 A steelworks. ....

5 An advertising agency. ....

a) Nearness to the target market	**v)** Excellent, traffic-free access to motorways
b) Nearness to raw materials	**w)** No direct competitor nearby
c) Plentiful supply of low-wage labour	**x)** Good access to staff with the right skills
d) Located near to rival firms	**y)** Close to an international airport
e) Good housing and schools nearby	**z)** Government grants available in Assisted Areas

D Data response

Jape plc has outgrown its headquarters and wants to relocate. It has shortlisted two sites: Derby and Coventry. Coventry is near enough to the current site to mean that about 25% of staff would be able to commute. Others would have to leave and be replaced. Only 10% could commute to Derby. Sandy Jape, Deputy Managing Director, has gathered the following data on the sites.

		Derby	Coventry
One-off costs	Site purchase	£2,250,000	£2,900,000
	Building and decor	£1,200,000	£1,150,000
	Redundancies	£1,050,000	£950,000
Running costs (annual)	Rates and bills	£800,000	£750,000
	Salaries	£4,800,000	£4,500,000
	Travel and expenses	£600,000	£700,000

1 How much higher are the one-off costs of siting in Coventry? ....

2 Calculate the difference between the running costs at the two proposed sites, then calculate the pay-back period of the Coventry site compared with Derby.

....

....

3 Using the differences between the two sites, draw up a cash flow table to calculate the average rate of return of investing in Coventry rather than Derby. Base your calculations on a five year period.

....

....

....

....

....

4 Outline two qualitative factors that might lead Jape plc to prefer Derby to Coventry.

....

....

....

Management By Objectives

A Missing words

Management By Objectives (MBO) is at the heart of a d... leadership style.

If a leader delegates a... (decision-making power) to five junior managers, s/he must be confident that they will not head off in five different directions. In other words, delegation requires careful coordination, and that is best achieved by agreeing clear targets (o...) from the start. The leader must be clear on the corporate objective and then break it down into sub-objectives for each manager. The key thing then is to ensure that the managers believe their own targets are achievable (however challenging). This is best achieved by consultation on the targets before they are set.

B Valid or invalid?

Are the following criticisms of MBO valid or invalid? Briefly explain your answer.

1 MBO leads to increased levels of bureaucracy within an organisation.

....

....

2 Will be ineffective if the manager cannot control key elements affecting the achievement of targets.

....

....

3 Subordinates may negotiate objectives that are quite easy to achieve.

....

....

4 MBO may weaken business ethics, as lines of responsibility become fuzzy.

....

....

5 The pressure to meet objectives is likely to be excessively stressful for staff.

....

....

C Explain two

1 Reasons why MBO may aid staff motivation. ....

....

2 Reasons why individual objectives should be discussed and agreed, not just set by the boss. ....

....

3 Risks, if the boss and the manager do not meet regularly to discuss progress.

....

....

D Data response

Simpson's Bank has been a leading merchant bank for 260 years.

Two years ago it branched out into offering personal pensions and insurance-linked savings schemes to the public. The new business started slowly but satisfactorily, until the Managing Director's new management by objectives policy led to very ambitious targets for the Sales Director. Within six months, sales rocketed by 120%, making the Pensions and Savings Division the most profitable within Simpson's.

A few months later, the MD received a hostile letter from a long-standing customer who was furious about being sold a pension scheme that an expert friend has described as: 'a lousy scheme for anyone, but especially for you'. The MD simply passed the letter on to Sales. A full six months later, a big article in *The Sunday Times* was followed by a 'Watchdog' TV assassination of the 'poor products sold irresponsibly to the wrong people by an over-enthusiastic sales force'.

1 The Sales Director felt unconcerned about the ethics of his department's approach; he felt his duty was simply to achieve the objectives set. Should he have felt morally responsible? Explain your answer.

....

....

....

2 The Managing Director did not feel responsible for what had happened because he did not know the details of what was going on. Is that a valid reason, given the MBO policy?

....

....

....

Management reorganisation during growth

A Missing words

Growth not only places a strain on cash .... , it also makes the task of management much harder. As rising sales force a firm to hire more people, spans of control .... , perhaps to the point where control and supervision suffer. In response a firm may introduce new .... of management, but this causes new problems with .... , two-way communication and also teamwork.

Underlying everything is the possibility that the dynamic .... who started the business may lack the skills to manage it successfully as it expands into a large company.

B Draw arrows to match cause to effect

Cause	Effect
1 A new layer of management added	a) Loss of management control
2 Widening span of control	b) Insufficient delegation to new managers
3 Careful, detailed selection and training of new staff	c) Senior staff may compete too fiercely with each other
4 New structure created, with product directors	d) Risk of loss of shared vision
5 Autocratic entrepreneur	e) Weaker customer focus due to time spent on staff

C State two possible management problems in each of the following circumstances

1 A new product launched by a small software company results in a company-wide growth rate of 20% per month.

....

....

....

2 C. Coleman's new internet business grows very rapidly, forcing him to expand staffing from 2 to 42 in six months.

....

....

....

D Which terms are defined by the following statements?

1 The number of staff answerable directly to a supervisor or manager.

....

2 Passing authority down the hierarchy.

....

3 A system of management that checks all decisions and ensures that decisions, actions and information are recorded with care and conform to pre-set rules.

....

4 A fluid management system in which staff can work on projects for more than one boss.

....

E Briefly explain why

1 There is a risk of loss of direction and control when a small firm is growing very rapidly.

....

....

2 Good entrepreneurs can struggle to become good managers.

....

....

....

Examiners' Notes

This is often an underlying theme in exam cases, because it is known to be a big test of leadership. Can the entrepreneur change to become a leader/manager instead of the king of a small empire?

Market conditions

A Missing words

A key influence upon a firm's success is the nature of demand and competition within its market. If all the rival firms are suffering from .... capacity, they will be tempted to correct the shortfall in demand by .... prices to attract customers. This can make it difficult or even impossible to make a profit.

At least as important is the market structure – is there one dominant supplier (a ....) or do many small suppliers compete? Where one firm dominates (e.g. Microsoft) it may be very hard to get your own new product established.

B State the terms defined by the following

1 A market in which two firms dominate sales.   ....

2 A situation in which demand is outstripping
   firms' ability to supply.   ....

3 A market dominated by a few large firms.   ....

4 A market where many small firms compete
   in selling identical products.   ....

C Data response

Look at this data on the market for computer keyboards, then answer the questions below.

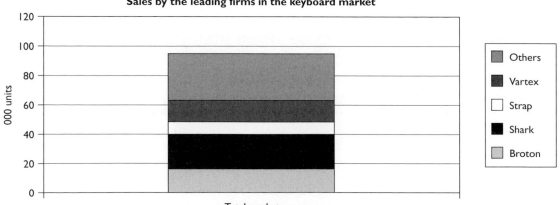

Sales by the leading firms in the keyboard market

92

1 Total capacity in the keyboard market is 120,000 units. Total sales are currently 95,000 units. How might this situation be viewed by a medium-sized producer such as Vartex?

    ....

    ....

    ....

2 The marketing director of Shark has heard that Broton is about to offer price discounts and longer credit periods to retailers. State two reasons why Shark might choose *not* to respond.

    ....

    ....

    ....

3 When Strap entered the market two years ago with an innovative niche market product, Shark slashed its prices on its rival keyboards, to try to stop Strap establishing itself. What is the term used to describe this business behaviour?

    ....

Examiners' **Notes**

Case studies often present a picture of business triumph which is in fact a consequence of favourable market conditions, e.g. the 1997–2000 economic boom; a downturn cuts utilisation and can quickly turn a business into a loss maker. Market conditions should always be considered with care.

Markets and competition

A Missing words

When annual profits are high, chief executives like to applaud the success of their business strategies. In poor years, the fault is often said to lie with 'market conditions', 'disorderly markets' or even – in the case of Richard Branson's Virgin Group – 'dirty tricks' by competitors. In reality, in a business such as running an airline, good or bad years depend largely on factors outside the control of management. .... capacity on the London–New York route may be forcing prices down. Or a new competitor's bid for market share may be forcing you to .... your prices in response.

B True or false?

Place a T or an F by each of the following statements.

1 Capacity shortage within an industry might lead prices to fall sharply. ☐

2 Penetration pricing by a new firm would be regarded legally as unfair competition. ☐

3 An oligopoly marketplace is one in which a few firms have a dominant market position. ☐

4 A cartel agreement to fix prices is nowadays regarded as fair competition. ☐

C Fair or unfair?

Put an F or a U by each of the following.

1 Fierce cost cutting followed by undercutting the prices charged by competitors. ☐

2 Spreading rumours about the financial health of a rival. ☐

3 Insisting that retailers stock your whole product range, not just your best-sellers. ☐

4 Offering big discounts to retailers who agree to stock your new product. ☐

5 Hacking into your rivals' computer systems to obtain their customer contact details. ☐

6 Refusing to supply retailers who sell your products at below the recommended price. ☐

7 Featuring your competitors in your advertising by making direct performance comparisons. ☐

8 Cutting your price in one area of the country, to prevent a new local rival from getting established. ☐

D Fill in the gaps

1 A .... is a single firm with a dominant market position.

2 In early 2001 a capacity .... in the UK housing market forced prices up.

3 The UK market for detergents is dominated by two firms; this situation is known as a ....

4 Cost cutting and price cutting are features of a competition that is fierce but ....

E Data response

The privatisation of bus services in the 1990s led to many instances of local 'bus wars' in which well-financed, national operators ran extra – sometimes free – services on bus routes until the smaller local firm abandoned the route.

1 Is this competition fair or unfair? Briefly explain why.

....

....

2 What is likely to happen after the local firm has given up the route?

....

....

3 Briefly explain whether you think the government should intervene to stop this from happening.

....

....

Examiners' Notes

Firms hate competition, but without it they can quickly become complacent and inward-looking (ignoring the customer). Many are quick to shout that competition is 'unfair' when it is fierce, but fair. This makes it hard for the Office of Fair Trading to spot the really anti-competitive practices.

Market size, growth and share

A Missing words

Market size can be measured by value (the value of all the .... made by all the companies in a market) or by .... (the quantity of sales made in a marketplace). These figures enable firms to look at their own sales as a % of the total market, i.e. their market .... If the whole market is enjoying sales growth, each firm is likely to benefit from rising revenues and the opening up of new opportunities.

B Draw arrows to match cause to effect

Cause	Effect
1 Price rises throughout a market lead to small reductions in demand	a) Rise in market size by value
2 Rival firms launch new products that revitalise sales within a market	b) Market size rising by value, but falling in volume
3 Sales volumes rise due to greater demand, not price cutting	c) Growth in market share
4 A brand becomes trendy, having been worn by the star of a TV soap	d) Sale decline for a year, though the market may still be set for long-term growth
5 A sharp recession cuts sales of luxury goods	e) Your own brand's sales are static, but market share is declining

C Briefly explain the business significance of

1 Market size growing by volume but staying static by value.

....

....

2 Rapid growth within one segment of a static market.

....

....

3   Becoming market leader, i.e. the brand with the largest market share.

....

....

....

D Data response

Look at these sales figures for brands of potting compost, then answer the questions below.

Brands	2 years ago	Last year	This year
Lexington	£5,600,000	£6,250,000	£6,350,000
Darton	£2,350,000	£2,750,000	£2,950,000
All others	£8,050,000	£7,500,000	£7,200,000
Total market	£16,000,000	£16,500,000	£16,500,000

1   The average price per bag of compost this year is £3.30. Calculate the market size by volume.

....

2   Calculate the market share of Lexington two years ago and this year.

....

....

3   Calculate the % sales growth in Darton since two years ago, and compare this with the % market growth over the same period.

....

4   Briefly comment on whether Lexington or Darton has been the more successful brand over the past two years.

....

....

....

....

Examiners' Notes

Be clear to distinguish between size, growth and share of the market; and recognise that a small share of a huge market may generate far more revenue than a large share of a small market (e.g. Kit-Kat has a far higher annual turnover than Manchester United plc).

Marketing mix

A Missing words

The marketing mix is the way in which a firm puts into practice its marketing
s............................... .

The mix of product, p......................... , promotion and place must be coordinated within
a strategy that can meet the firm's marketing o..................................... .The heart of a
successful mix is a product that meets customer needs, wants and spending power.

B Which marketing element belongs with which P?

Write **a)**, **b)**, **c)** or **d)** by each of the numbered marketing elements

a) Product	**b)** Price	**c)** Promotion	**d)** Place

1 Skimming the market ....   7 Market penetration ....

2 Above the line ....   8 Prominent in-store display ....

3 Distribution targets ....   9 Protective packaging ....

4 Media advertising ....   10 Eye-catching packaging ....

5 Blind taste test ....   11 Cost-plus ....

6 Branding ....   12 Sponsoring sports events ....

C Identify the following definitions, then find the word formed from the first letter of each one

1 How a launch marketing strategy can be assessed
in a real, if local, area.   ....

2 Testing and developing the product to see
how to improve it.   ....

3 The most common form of above-the-line
promotion.   ....

4 Pricing the same product at different prices for
different people.   ....

5 A number that shows the relationship between
demand and a variable that affects demand.   ....

Answer ....

D Data response

Look at the data for Cardews Chocolates, then answer the questions.

	This year	Last year
Advertising spending	£8.5 million	£9.0 million
Spending on sales promotions	£2.8 million	£1.8 million
Share of chocolate market	29.9%	29.4%

1 What hypothesis can be drawn from the above data?

....

....

2 How could that hypothesis be tested?

....

....

3 Why might Cardews' approach prove to be a mistake, if its objective was to build market share steadily to 32% over the next five years?

....

....

E Tough, but crucial, A2 questions

Give two answers to each.

1 How might a firm's marketing mix be affected by shortage of capacity?

....

....

....

2 How might Walls evaluate the effectiveness of its marketing plan for a newly launched ice cream?

....

....

....

3 How might Walls' personnel and operations functions be affected by a marketing decision to relaunch Cornetto as a premium priced, upmarket product?

....

....

....

Marketing objectives and strategy

A Missing words

Marketing .... is the plan for meeting your marketing goals or
.... The objectives are set after assessing trends and competition
within the market, usually by company directors.

Strategy may also be set at the same level of seniority, or may be delegated from the
directors to senior managers. In the latter case, the managers will need to return to
the .... to get approval for the financial and staffing resources
needed to give the strategy a chance to succeed.

It should always be remembered, though, that just as only one in five new products
succeeds, so will many – perhaps most – marketing strategies fail to meet their
.... This is because if a great opportunity exists, several
companies may decide to aim for the same goal – meaning, perhaps, that no one can
successfully make a profit.

B Objective or strategy?

Place an O or an S by each of the following to show whether it is an objective
or a strategy.

1 To concentrate media spending on cinema advertising. ☐

2 To boost consumer awareness to above 50%. ☐

3 Establish a younger, trendier image. ☐

4 Price competitively during the launch period. ☐

5 To focus the budget on below-the-line activity. ☐

6 To boost market share to over 15%. ☐

7 To cut media spending to provide more resources for new product
development. ☐

8 To ensure a fully coordinated marketing mix. ☐

9 To maximise the profit made by declining brands. ☐

10 Achieve distribution in more than 70% of outlets. ☐

C Briefly explain why

1 Objectives should not be too ambitious.

....

2 The product is usually the most important element in the marketing mix.

....

....

3 Strategic decisions are made at very senior levels of management.

....

....

4 Failure to meet an objective may not mean the strategy was wrong

....

....

D Data response

Lennox Jewellers of Manchester was making huge profits from selling 'Posh and Becks' loyalty rings for £95 per pair. Mr Lennox decided to expand by opening other outlets in Leeds, Birmingham and Bristol. His approach was to appoint local managers and finance the expansion entirely by borrowings. After ten months his accountant urged him to rethink, as, 'It's cost you £1,200,000 so far and I don't think it'll ever prove successful.'

Mr Lennox closed down his new outlets and grieved over his huge losses.

1 What was Mr Lennox's objective? ....

2 Identify two possible weaknesses of his strategy. ....

....

3 Do you think he failed due to wrong objectives or the wrong strategy? Briefly explain your reasoning.

....

....

Examiners' Notes

To succeed, marketing objectives must fit in with the wider business objectives, and be carried through using a well-resourced strategy that makes the best use of the firm's strengths/assets.

Mission

A Missing words

Mission is a sense of purpose so strong that it compares with the zeal of a missionary. It is very unlikely to stem from an objective such as .... maximisation, as this has no higher purpose. Staff at the Co-op Bank, however, may work with enthusiasm, even fanaticism, as they push forward the bank's successful ethical policy.

During the 'dot.com' boom of 1999 and 2000, new start-ups showed a similar sense of mission as they rushed forward to try to change the face of business. This is a reminder that mission can motivate, but it can only succeed if the underlying s.......................... is sound.

Firms that lack a sense of mission may try to create one by writing out a mission ....

B Draw arrows to match the mission statement to the company

1 An arm's length from desire		a) Body Shop
2 A PC on every desk, worldwide		b) B.A.A.
3 To dedicate our business to the pursuit of social and environmental change		c) Coca-Cola
4 To become the world's most successful airport business		d) Virgin
5 To build through empowerment		e) Microsoft

C True or false?

Place a T or an F by each of the following statements.

1 An organisation's culture stems from staff attitudes and actions taken over many years.

2 A new mission – well explained – will change organisational culture quite quickly.

3 A new mission can be captured by an organisation's culture, which may be resistant to change.

4 If a new mission does capture the hearts and minds of staff, the culture will adjust.

D Will these missions succeed or fail? Explain why

1   To become the most profitable supermarket retailer in Britain. I judge that it would succeed/fail, because

    ....

    ....

    ....

2   To become the ethical supplier of cat food. I judge it would succeed/fail, because

    ....

    ....

    ....

E Influences on the success of a firm's mission statement

Read each of the following questions, then choose which one(s) you think the most important for Railtrack, if it decided its new mission would be 'Safety First'. Briefly explain your reasoning.

1   Is it a paper exercise or does it really affect the attitudes and behaviour of senior management?

2   Does it lead the business in a direction customers want?

3   Is the new mission absorbed within – or rejected by – the organisational culture?

....

....

....

....

Examiners' Notes

Do not muddle mission with aims; a mission should appeal to a higher purpose, such as 'to promote a healthier lifestyle'.

Monetary policy

A Missing words

Monetary policy has become the British government's main tool for influencing the short- to medium-term progress of the economy.

Although the .... of the Exchequer is responsible, the policy itself is conducted by the Bank of ....'s semi-independent Monetary Policy Committee. The MPC meets every month to decide on the level of interest rates. The MPC's brief is to keep inflation at around 2.5%. If there is a threat of higher inflation, interest rates will be pushed .... , to dampen down demand in the economy and therefore reduce prices. If inflation seems likely to fall below 2.5%, the MPC may cut the rate of interest to 'reflate' the economy.

B Why oh why?

1 Why might a cut in interest rates push up the rate of inflation?

....

....

2 Why might a small building firm be delighted to hear of a cut in interest rates?

....

....

3 Why might a government be worried about deflation (prices actually falling, year on year)?

....

....

4 Why might banks benefit from a higher interest rate set by the MPC?

....

....

C True or false?

Place a T or an F by each of the following statements.

1 A reduction in interest rates will reduce consumer spending and therefore inflation.

2   A rise in interest rates tends to increase the value of the £ because wealthy foreign savers buy pounds in order to enjoy the higher interest rates available in UK banks. ☐

3   The MPC is likely to cut interest rates if they believe a recession is looming. ☐

4   A rise in interest rates will tend to increase business investment. ☐

5   If Britain joins the Euro, UK interest rates will be set in Europe, not Britain. ☐

D Effects of monetary policy decisions

Complete each of the following by writing 'up' or 'down' in the gaps.

1   Interest rates up, value of the £ ....

2   Interest rates down, unemployment ....

3   Interest rates up, company investment ....

4   Interest rates down, consumer spending ....

E Distinguish carefully between

1   Lower interest rates   *and*   Lower exchange rates

....

....

2   Monetary policy   *and*   Fiscal policy

....

....

3   Falling inflation   *and*   Deflation

....

....

Examiners' **Notes**

Although the Bank of England's committee sets the interest rate, do not doubt that the government still has a major influence on what the rate will be.

Motivation 1. Theory

A Missing words

Motivation matters for the profit-focused reason that labour costs are too expensive to waste due to low .... (efficiency) or high labour .... It also matters for the ethical reason that managers should feel a duty to promote job satisfaction among staff.

Yet motivation should not be confused with movement. Herzberg says that .... means doing something because you want a reward or seek to avoid punishment; .... means doing something because you want to. The latter is desirable, because then people give of their best.

B Who's who?

Give the name of the person who formulated each of the following theories.

1 Two factor theory ....

2 Hierarchy of needs ....

3 Economic man ....

4 Theory of managerial attitudes ....

5 Human relations ....

C Circle the odd one out

1	X	Y	Z
2	Pay	Responsibility	Achievement
3	Group norms	Social needs	Unofficial leaders
4	Specialisation	Piece-rate	Self-actualisation

D Anagrams

1 Satisfied after your physicals   NO SAD SLICEE

....

2 A consequence of taking an interest   AHHR, O NEWT

....

3 Founder of 'scientific management'   FOWL TRAY

....

E What's wrong?

Briefly state the error contained within each of these statements.

1 Theory X workers can be motivated by good pay.

....

....

2 You can motivate people by offering them performance-related pay.

....

....

3 Mayo's hierarchy puts social needs above physical ones.

....

....

4 McGregor's theory of motivation was developed during the 1950s.

....

....

Examiners' Notes

For AS exams make sure you understand each of the theorists. For A2, a good understanding of one or two theories will be enough (Herzberg plus McGregor would be a good choice).

Motivation 2. In practice

A Missing words

Motivation is widely written about, yet many managers think it is just common sense. In fact, successfully motivating others is one of the most demanding and rewarding managerial skills.

In the 1980s and 1990s, performance- .... pay became fashionable first in British businesses, then government departments. At Board level, share o.. provided increasingly massive rewards for success – even modest success. Among middle managers and shopfloor staff, performance-related pay yielded far lower rewards – perhaps no more than 4 or 5%. Unsurprisingly, Directors received increasing criticism for being 'fat cats' (drinking all the cream), while more junior staff found little to motivate them in a few percentage points of extra salary.

B Identify the following definitions, then find the word formed from the first letter of each one

1 Paying staff per item they produce.   ....

2 Delegating power for staff to set their own objectives and methods, plus the resources to achieve them.   ....

3 Giving staff a legal stake in the company's equity.   ....

4 Encouraging staff to work and cooperate together, rather than acting in isolation.   ....

Answer ....

C Explain why

1 Higher pay may not lead to higher motivation.

....

....

2 A profit share within a large organisation may be ineffective.

....

....

3 Some staff may dislike teamworking.

....

....

D Data response

Having learnt about motivation theory in her A Level, Sonal Shah was shocked by her first few weeks working at the Home Office.

This huge government department seemed full of people working in isolation, but with astonishingly low productivity and enthusiasm. Tea breaks, lunch breaks or departmental meetings all yielded the same moans about the difficulties and frustrations of their jobs. In fact, most seemed quite comfortable to Sonal. None was remotely as hard-worked or as pressured as those at Sonal's previous jobs at Dixons and at a toy factory.

As a graduate trainee she was expected to write a 5,000-word report on a subject of her own choosing. Staff were not pleased to hear that she chose 'Poor Motivation in the HRM department'.

1 a) Identify two indicators of low morale in the text.

....

b) State two possible reasons for this low morale.

....

2 Identify two possible benefits from establishing more teamwork in the department.

....

....

3 Sonal's view is that there is a need for job enrichment, but the department manager prefers to consider job rotation. Explain why Sonal might be right.

....

....

Examiners' Notes

Deep down, most students believe money motivates; remember that this is true for some (especially student part-time workers) but by no means all. Beware of over-generalising about people.

Moving averages

A Missing words

Data such as sales figures can vary wildly from month to month, depending on factors such as the actions of c... . To get a clear picture of success or failure, therefore, it is important to identify underlying trends. This can be done by calculating the .... average of the data.

If sales are affected by seasonal factors, a 12-month moving average will be needed. For instance, with toy sales it is vital that every calculation should include one D.. . Comparing quarterly data (July to September and October to December, for example) would be pointless, as the dominance of Christmas sales would mean sales jump ahead in the winter quarter.

B Calculating moving averages

Worked example: 2-month moving average of sales of Marmite (all figures in £000s)

	Monthly sales	Moving total	Moving average
January	£2,100		
February	£2,250		£2,183 (Jan–March)
March	£2,200	£6,550	£2,200 (Feb–April)
April	£2,150	£6,600	£2,217 (March–May)
May	£2,300	£6,650	£2,250 (April–June)
June	£2,300	£6,750	

1 Now you calculate a 3-month moving average based on these sales of A-Z Handbooks (in units).

	Monthly sales	Moving total	Moving average
January	£ 875		
February	£1,250		
March	£1,050		
April	£ 775		
May	£ 980		
June	£1,470		

C Making use of trend information

Label each statement with a U for useful or an S for useless.

1 For forecasting sales in six months' time. ☐

2 For setting budgets. ☐

3 For constructing a Profit and Loss Account. ☐

4 For predicting the path of a product life cycle. ☐

5 For calculating the effect of an advertising campaign. ☐

6 For identifying personnel indicators that are improving or worsening, e.g absenteeism. ☐

7 For estimating future capacity needs. ☐

8 For assessing whether budgets have been met. ☐

D Briefly explain which time period would be best for calculating a moving average (e.g. three months), for each of the following situations

1 Swimwear sales.

....

2 A new soap powder launched three months ago.

....

....

3 A rapidly growing brand with sales that are erratic, but not seasonal.

....

....

....

Examiners' Notes

Moving averages are a useful way to show underlying trends, but should be treated with caution, especially if used to extrapolate the future. As with all statistics, ask who is providing the data and why.

Niche v. mass marketing

A Missing words

Mass marketing targets a product at the heart of a market, aiming to achieve an acceptable (perhaps quite small) % .... of a large sales total.

By contrast, niche marketing aims to develop or enter a relatively small sector, but to enjoy sales dominance within it. This process of segmentation may also lead to increases in market .... , as tailoring new products to specific types of customer can make them increase their rate of purchasing, e.g. the launch of adult-focused crisps such as Kettle Chips increased the whole market for salted snacks.

B Match the benefit to the category

Write in letters below.

1 Mass marketing ....

2 Niche marketing ....

a) Upward sales potential is huge	**e)** Can charge quite high prices
b) Costs can be spread over large sales volumes	**f)** Important to establish high consumer recognition
c) Little or no competition	**g)** Price elasticity likely to be low
d) Important to achieve high distribution levels	**h)** May expand the market size

C Explain why

1 Product differentiation is especially important in mass markets.

....

....

2 Small firms find it easier to compete by niche marketing.

....

....

3 Mass-marketed products are likely to have high price elasticity.

....

....

D Data response

Look at the data below, then answer the questions.

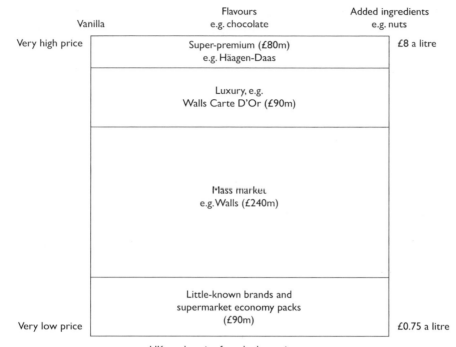

UK market size for take-home ice cream:
approx. £500m a year

The American ice-cream maker Mattus is considering launching into Britain. It has carried out a market segmentation analysis and must now decide whether to launch into the super-premium market or the mass market.

1 Mattus believes it can get a 10% share of the super-premium sector. What is that worth in sales per year?

....

2 In the mass market it believes it could reach a 5% share. Explain two reasons why that may prove less profitable than 10% of super-premium?

....

....

....

Opportunity cost

A Missing words

Opportunity cost is the cost of missing out on the next best opportunity when making a ....

The usual way to put a figure on opportunity cost is to use the .... rate, i.e. the cost of missing out on the interest available from money held in a deposit account. It is important to remember that every business decision has a cost (in money, time or other resources) and must therefore be weighed up with care.

B When are opportunity costs relevant?

Write 'Yes' or 'No' by each of the following.

1 When a choice must be made? ....

2 When luck may influence a result? ....

3 When a decision is called for? ....

C What might be the opportunity cost when

1 You spend an evening doing homework.

....

2 The government increases spending on the NHS by £5 billion.

....

3 Marks & Spencer buys an American chain of clothing stores for £1.5 billion.

....

4 A firm allows its credit control to slip, so customers take 50% longer to pay their bills.

....

....

D Mini-mini case

After running out of ingredients for its lunchtime specials, a restaurant has decided to increase its stock levels by 50%. Which of the following are *actual* costs that might be incurred and which are *opportunity* costs?

1 Higher interest charges. ....

2 Less finance available for other uses. ....

3 Higher wastage levels. ....

4 Less able to offer customers credit. ....

Examiners' Notes

Think about opportunity costs every time you use the word 'decision'.

Think about opportunity costs every time you are asked about: control of working capital, stock control; quality control; marketing spending; training.

Avoid the trap of assuming that money is tight in small firms, but large firms do things because they 'can afford to'. In fact, large firms are often more focused upon opportunity costs and are therefore *more* careful about wasting resources.

Organisational structure

A Missing words

All organisations have management hierarchies arranged as a pyramid, with one (occasionally two) people at the top and then management layers that become more numerous as they get closer to the shop floor.

If the .... of control is wide, relatively few managers will be needed at each level; therefore not many layers will be needed. Whereas a .... span of control will require many managers, many layers and therefore a severe risk of over-supervision and b...y.

cont.

cont. Organisations also tend to have a departmental structure. This might be based upon products (Birds Eye frozen vegetables; Birds Eye frozen desserts etc.), upon regions or even countries. Most common of all, though, is to organise by business function. The most common of these .... are: marketing, finance, operations management and IT.

B Draw arrows to match the statement to the term

Statement	Term
1 A person who communication passes through, on route to its target (the receiver)	a) Functional organisation
2 Forming project teams from a number of departments, thereby making staff answerable to two bosses (the project leader and their own department head)	b) Intermediary
3 Dividing a business into operational departments such as marketing, finance and HRM	c) Delayering
4 Cutting out one tier of management, to speed up decision making and vertical communication	d) Matrix management

C Fill in the missing numbers

See diagram on facing page.

1 A managing director with the organisational hierarchy shown in the diagram has a span of control of ....

2 Below the managing director level, what is the average span of control in this organisation? ....

3 Research has shown that communication effectiveness falls by 25% with every intermediary the message passes through. If a managing director's message must pass through 4 intermediaries before reaching shopfloor staff, only .... % of the effectiveness will remain.

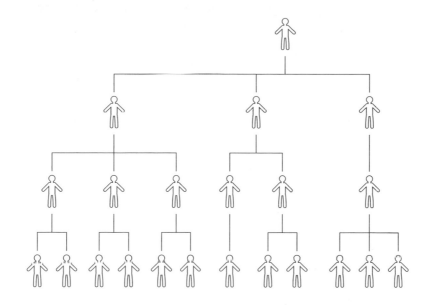

D Give two reasons why

1 Delayering may damage an organisation.

....

2 A narrow span of control may prove effective.

....

....

3 Japanese firms favour 'horizontal promotion', in which staff move from one functional area/department to another, receiving a pay rise even though they have not yet risen to a higher management layer.

....

....

....

Examiners' **Notes**

Healthy organisations are not concerned or even aware of structure and hierarchy; staff work under their own initiative and talk to bosses and subordinates as friends and colleagues. In large, bureaucratic businesses, though, lines of authority and accountability are a matter of huge concern. More is the pity.

Personnel effectiveness

A Missing words

> Successful human .... management (HRM) relies upon measuring and controlling staff performance in quantifiable ways such as productivity, labour .... , a................................... and health and ....
> This is because the basis of HRM is the implicit promise that personnel can be planned for, and managed, as efficiently as other resources such as materials and components.
>
> At the start of the year a workforce plan will predict the number of staff needed; this will require predictions of labour productivity (e................................) and absence levels. HR managers will then be very keen to ensure that the actual figures prove no worse than expected.

B True or false?

Place a T or an F by each of the following statements.

1 Absenteeism is highest among staff on lower grades within organisations. ☐

2 Labour turnover varies with the business cycle, i.e. high in booms; low in recessions. ☐

3 Labour productivity is highest in recessions, when people are in fear of their jobs. ☐

4 Health and safety data such as accidents per worker are always published in company annual reports. ☐

C Formulae

Fill in the gaps.

1 Labour turnover is measured by the formula:

$$\frac{\text{Number of staff leaving in the year}}{\text{...}} \times 100$$

2 Absenteeism is measured by the formula:

$$\frac{\text{Number of days ....}}{\text{Total staff days during the time period}} \times 100$$

3 Labour productivity is output divided by the number of .... It shows output per worker.

D Data response

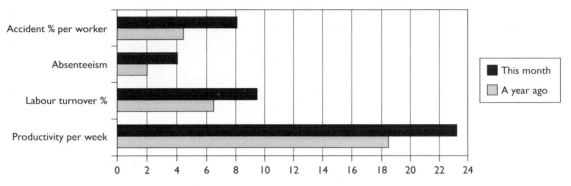

Personnel indicators at JNC Plastics Ltd

1 From the bar chart, outline one factor that may be beneficial to profit and one that may be damaging it.

....

....

2 During the year, union membership at JNC Plastics has risen from 32% of staff to 47%. Suggest two possible reasons why.

....

....

3 JNC's profit this year has risen by 34% and shareholders are thrilled. Why may the longer-term profit potential look more worrying?

....

....

....

Examiners' Notes

Exam answers about people at work can easily become waffly. Useful, then, to relate issues such as morale to measurable criteria such as productivity or labour turnover.

Practical problems of start-ups

A Missing words

Starting a small business is easy to do, but very hard to do well. As many as 40% of new firms fail to survive their first year of trading.

The main problem is building a customer base, i.e. sufficient regular trade to operate above ....–even. Exceptionally, trade can be fantastic, if the product becomes fashionable from the start. When this happens, there remains a risk that excessively rapid growth may cause .... flow problems as the firm tries to expand capacity.

Although a good .... plan should help prevent major errors, there is little evidence that it is becoming safer to start a new firm.

B Financing the early stages

Draw arrows to match the type of business to the financial problem that may be faced.

Type of business start-up	Financial problem
1 A new manufacturer of micro-waveable Mexican meals that aims to sell to the major supermarket chains	**a)** Hard to raise the start-up capital required to make the business seem credible from the outset
2 A new insurance company founded by the former Chief Executive of a major banking group	**b)** Start-up costs may be huge in relation to the likely sales turnover of the business
3 A new, independent clothes shop specialising in designer fashion clothes	**c)** Building a customer base will be difficult as there is no cheap way to reach the target market
4 A student who has left college early to set up an internet site selling exam advice from chief examiners!	**d)** Cash flow may be a severe problem because of lengthy credit periods expected by retail customers

C Location, location, location

Explain why

1   A kebab shop paying a rent of £3,500 a month for a City centre site may be getting a bargain, even though there are sites available elsewhere for £800 a month.

....

....

2 New small retail firms find it hard to persuade property developers to let them rent prime sites.

....

....

3 Clever retailers check the pedestrian traffic count at a site before negotiating a rent with the landlord.

....

....

4 New manufacturing firms need to check on the speed and efficiency of road access before making a location decision.

....

....

D Data response

JBM Cars plans to import American cars and sports vehicles, convert them to right-hand drive, then sell them at prices between £10,000 and £18,000. JB himself has written a full business plan, but raising £240,000 from the bank is proving difficult. JB is angry because, 'We shareholders have shown our faith by investing £50,000. Why is the bank holding us up?'

1 Identify three reasons why the bank may be reluctant.

....

....

....

2 Identify two problems JBM may have in building a customer base.

....

....

Examiners' Notes

Exam answers tend to focus too much on finance. The hardest thing is to identify a market opportunity big enough, profitable enough and sufficiently long lasting to build a successful business.

Pricing methods

A Missing words

Firms set prices in line with their perception of what the market will bear and in relation to their marketing o.. .

When Virgin Atlantic was launched in 1984, £99 fares were offered to New York, both to attract media attention and to achieve market p... .
When British Airways cut its prices later that year, Richard Branson accused it of p... pricing.

Most everyday pricing decisions hinge on whether the product is a price leader or a price t........................... . The latter forces the firm to price at, or below, the level decided on by other firms – often the price leader.

B Match two characteristics to each way of setting price

1 Cost plus ....   2 Psychological ....   3 Discrimination ....

4 Skimming ....   5 Predatory ....   6 Penetration ....

a) Aims to push weaker rivals out of the market	**u)** Pricing low to achieve a market share breakthrough
b) Pricing high for maximum margins	**v)** Only works if customers cannot trade with each other
c) Pricing differently for different customers	**w)** Only works if there is no effective competition
d) If proved, breaks competition laws	**x)** Explains all those £9,995 car prices
e) Adding a profit % to unit costs	**y)** Based on hoping that prices can be increased later
f) Pricing based on consumer perceptions	**z)** May help establish top quality image

C Briefly distinguish between

1 Loss leader pricing *and* Penetration pricing

....

....

....

2 Cost plus pricing *and* Skimming the market

....

....

....

3 Pricing methods *and* Pricing tactics

....

....

....

D Calculations

1 A business with sales of 2,000 products a week and fixed costs of £8,000 decides to price on the basis of a 25% mark up. Its variable costs per unit are £4.20.

a) Calculate the selling price.

....

....

b) If the business chose then to allow for psychological price barriers, what price should be set? ....

2 A brand's price elasticity is known to be about 0.5, but when its price is increased from £9.75 to £10.25, sales fall by 12%.

a) What is the price elasticity now?

....

b) Why is it different from usual?

....

Examiners' Notes

Whatever pricing method is chosen, the keys to success are to understand your product's position in the marketplace and ensure that your price fits in with the other factors in the marketing mix.

Primary research

A Missing words

> Primary research means obtaining evidence first hand, probably from potential or current customers. It can be gathered with a sufficiently large sample to be statistically valid (..................................... research) or be small-scale, in-depth (.....................................) research. Either way, it will be tailored to achieve specific objectives, such as to find the attitudes of existing customers to a potential change in pack design.

B Draw arrows to match the research method to the research objectives

Research objectives	Research method
1 To find what Galaxy buyers prefer about the chocolate	a) Quantitative survey based upon a random sample
2 To find what high-income women *really* think about Gucci	b) Matched samples of 200 consumers, to compare results based on slightly different questions
3 To find what % of vodka drinkers visit the cinema regularly	c) Conduct a blind product test on a 200 sample
4 To find what makes wholesale grocery outlets choose one biscuit brand instead of another	d) Hold a group discussion among AB social grade females
5 To test the impact upon demand of different prices charged for the same product	e) In-depth interviews carried out at the respondent's workplace

C Briefly explain the meaning of

1 Quota sample.

....

....

2 95% confidence level.

....

....

3 A statistically valid sample.

....

....

D *Spot eight mistakes in the following extract from a questionnaire (in a student project)*

1 Could you please tell me your age: .... years

2 Could you please tell me your sex: Male .... Female ....

3 How often do you buy organic vegetables?

Very often .... Quite often .... Not very often ....

4 What price premium do you usually pay for organic vegetables and what would you be prepared to pay?

30% or more ....

20–30% ....

10–20% ....

Up to 10% ....

5 Would you shop at a greengrocer that offered high-quality organic produce, with free home delivery, at no price premium?

Yes .... No ....

....

....

....

....

....

....

....

....

Examiners' **Notes**

Ideally, research is carried out by independent researchers on large, representative samples. But remember that this is expensive, so do not dismiss a small firm's smaller scale, less professional surveys.

Productivity

A Missing words

1 Productivity measures output per .... It is a measure of business
....

2 Productivity is affected by the level of .... in machinery and
equipment, the amount and quality of staff training, and the level of employee
....

3 If productivity rises when demand is unchanged, the likely consequence for staff
is a programme of ....

4 The formula for calculating productivity is $\dfrac{\rule{6cm}{0.4pt}}{\text{Number of staff employed}}$.

This shows output per worker.

B Calculations

1 Vartex employs 120 production staff. Their average earnings are £17,500 per year. This
year's output is expected to be 42,000 units.

   a) Calculate labour productivity at Vartex.

   b) Calculate the labour cost per unit.

2 A benchmarking exercise has shown that Vartex's most efficient competitor pays
£21,000 per year to its 80 staff. The staff produce a total annual output of 48,000 units.

   a) Calculate the competitor's labour productivity.

   b) Calculate the labour costs per unit for the competitor.

   c) Both firms price their goods at £59.00. Assuming there are no other costs, what
   profit per unit is made by each business?

C Cause and effect

Some of the following statements are causes and some are effects of low productivity at a business. Others are neither. Write a C by the causes or an E by the effects of low productivity and put an N by the others.

1 High labour costs per unit. ☐

2 High automation. ☐

3 Low profitability. ☐

4 Low morale among the workforce. ☐

5 High levels of re-working. ☐

6 Old machinery. ☐

7 Business is uncompetitive internationally. ☐

8 Poorly educated and trained workers. ☐

9 Prices may need to rise. ☐

10 Less labour required in the short term. ☐

D True or false?

Place a T or an F by each of the following statements.

1 Rising productivity is impossible without rising production. ☐

2 Rising productivity means fewer jobs, if demand/output remains static. ☐

3 Rising productivity means fewer jobs, but protects them in the longer term. ☐

4 Rising productivity will only help firms grow if demand increases. ☐

Examiners' Notes

This term is misused more than any other. Before using it, stop and think:

'Am I showing that I know the difference between productivity and production?' Remember: productivity measures the *efficiency* of production, *not* the quantity.

Product life cycle and product portfolio

A Missing words

> The theory of the product life cycle is that every product follows the same natural path through .... , growth, ... and decline. If the product/service stays the same, the last two stages are inevitable, says the theory, because of new innovations by .... and changing customer .... Therefore .... strategies are needed to prolong the profitable life span.
>
> The .... Matrix also looks at the stages in a product's life, but in relation to two variables: market growth and market .... The matrix is a way of assessing the prospects of the different products within a firm's portfolio. It helps to set priorities in marketing spending, e.g. to cut advertising on product A and use the cash to double the spend on the 'rising star' product B.

B Weaknesses

For each weakness, identify whether it refers to the Boston Matrix (BM) or the PLC.

1 Is a static model, i.e. does not show changes over time.   ....

2 In effect, treats all new products as problem children.   ....

3 May encourage management apathy (oh, it's in decline . . .).   ....

4 May encourage premature marketing cutbacks on top-selling products.   ....

5 Can only be 'correct' in hindsight, i.e. it has no predictive powers.   ....

C Identify the terms defined by

1 The Boston stage in which low market share combines with low market growth.

2 The point at which a firm is producing flat-out and cannot cope with extra demand.

3 The Boston stage where a product has a high share of a growing market.

4 A medium-term plan to prolong the profitable lifetime of a product.

D Briefly explain why

1 A cow is milked to help feed a problem child.

....

....

....

2 A rising star is given as many resources as a firm can afford.

....

....

....

3 It is necessary to develop new products while existing ones are in their growth stage.

....

....

....

4 Dogs may be withdrawn before their sales die completely.

....

....

5 'Buy One Get One Free' is *not* an extension strategy.

....

....

Examiners' Notes

Yes, you know the stages and the labels, but can you write a paragraph on the implications upon marketing and finance of each stage in the life cycle *and* the matrix? For example, what are the implications for marketing strategy of most of your products falling into the category 'cash cow'?

Profit

A Missing words

> Profit is the value of sales (revenue) minus the costs incurred in generating those sales (total costs). Revenue is the value of .... made within a time period (such as a financial year). It is calculated by the formula: Revenue = Sales volume × ....
>
> Total costs comprise the fixed overheads plus the total variable costs. These must be deducted from .... to give ....

B Calculations

1 If a firm sells 200 Widgets at £3.20 and 40 Squidgets at £4, what is its total revenue?

....

2 In the above example, each Widget costs £1.20 to make, while each Squidget costs £1.50. What are the total variable costs?

....

....

3 If fixed costs are £300, what profit is the business making?

....

C Explain exactly how the following changes would affect profit

1 A firm in a highly competitive industry increases its prices by 8%.

....

....

....

2 Demand for a firm's products falls sharply due to changing fashions.

....

....

....

3 New production methods increase a firm's factory reject rate.

....

....

....

D Calculations

At full capacity output of 24,000 units, a firm's costs are as follows:

managers' salaries	£48,000	materials	£12,000
rent and rates	£24,000	piece-rate labour	£36,000

1 What are the firm's total costs at 20,000 units?

....

....

....

....

2 What profit will be made at 20,000 units if the selling price is £6?

....

E Explain why

1 Profit per unit should rise when fuller use is made of a firm's capacity.

....

2 Cutting costs can boost short-term profit at the expense of the long term.

....

....

3 Cutting prices may not boost profit.

....

....

4 New small firms tend to concentrate more upon cash flow than profit.

....

....

Examiners' Notes

This is the most important calculation in the whole subject. Yet a surprising number of candidates forget to adjust total variable costs in line with changes in demand – and therefore work it out wrongly. Give yourself lots of practice on profit calculations.

Profit and Loss Accounts

A Missing words

A Profit and Loss Account shows revenues and .... for a past trading period; usually 12 months. It shows the trading position of the business, one-off profits or .... , the .... tax payable, the dividends decided upon by the .... and the bottom line, the .... profit. The quality of the profit is said to be high if it has largely come from ongoing trading, i.e. it can be expected to recur next year.

B Types of profit

Fill in the gaps.

1 Gross profit is sales turnover minus ....

2 Operating profit is gross profit minus ....

3 Pre-tax profit is operating profit + ...

4 Profit after tax is .... minus corporation tax.

5 Retained profit is profit after tax minus ....

C Identify two

1 Actions that would boost gross profit but may cut operating profit.

2 Reasons why a shareholder should worry if a firm's profit is low quality.

3 Ways that moving to JIT stock management might affect gross and operating profit.

4 Possible causes of substantial one-off profits or losses.

D Data response

	£000
Sales turnover	1,850
a)	b) ....
Gross profit	800
Overheads	640
c)	d) ....
One-off profits (losses)	200
Pre-tax profit	e) ....
Corporation tax (tax rate: 25%)	f) ....
Profit after tax	g) ....
Dividends	170
h)	100

1 Fill in the gaps **a–h**.

2 Would you consider the pre-tax profit to be high or low quality? Explain why.

....

3 Is the company wise to declare dividends of £170,000? Explain your answer.

....

....

Examiners' Notes

Is the profit shown in a company's published accounts a) a fact or b) an estimate? Is the profit made from selling a piece of property a) high quality or b) low quality? If you answered b) to both of these, take a bow. If you said a), please try the above questions again.

Profitability ratios

A Missing words

Profitability means measuring profit in relation to a yardstick, e.g. as a percentage of sales revenue. This helps in comparing the performances of firms of different sizes or in evaluating a firm's performance over time. It may be important to know the absolute size of a firm's profit, e.g. £1 million but has that been made from sales of £10 million or £100 million? The key ratios for measuring profitability are profit .... (profit as a percentage of sales) and .... on .... , which measures profit as a percentage of the capital invested in the business.

B Draw arrows to match the explanation to the statement

Statement	Explanation
1 Brital plc has made a return on capital of 16% this year compared with 14% last year	a) If margins are too high customers may question the value for money
2 'I'm thrilled that our restaurant has made a gross profit margin of 75% this year'	b) Some businesses have low profit margins, but still do well because of very high sales revenues
3 Five years ago, Marks & Spencer's net profit margin was double that of Tesco	c) ROC should be compared with the interest rate, but high-risk businesses should have very high returns
4 In a year when interest rates were 6%, VB Co. had a great year, making an ROC of 12%	d) A rise in ROC implies improved financial efficiency and performance of the business
5 BJP Co., wholesalers, has a net margin of just 2%	e) Gross margin has relatively little significance, because it ignores fixed overheads

C Formulae and calculations (1)

1 State the formula for the gross profit margin.

....

2   Net profit margin measures net profit as a percentage of sales. If a firm with annual sales of £600,000 has a net profit of £84,000, what is its net profit margin?

....

3   JC Co. has sales of £120,000 and profits of £12,000. Its capital employed is £75,000. Calculate the company's return on capital.

....

D True or false?

Place a T or an F by each of the following statements.

1   If ROC falls below the interest rate, highly geared firms are in very big trouble. ☐

2   If the gross margin rises, the net margin and ROC will *always* rise as well. ☐

3   Rising margins will lead to rising ROC, if asset turnover is unchanged. ☐

4   As a rule of thumb, an ROC of 100% implies that the firm should double in size every year. ☐

E Formulae and calculations (2)

1   If the net margin is 20% and the asset turnover is 2, what is the ROC?

....

2   ZQ Co. has sales of £4.2 million, costs of sales of £2.8m, overheads of £1.3m and corporation tax payments of £60,000. What is the company's gross margin?

....

....

3   If a firm with £1 million of sales has gross and net profit margins of 16% and 6% respectively, what are the firm's overhead costs?

....

....

Examiners' Notes

If you struggle to remember formulae, make return on capital your one profitability ratio. It is the most useful and the one examiners test most often.

Qualitative factors in financial decisions

A Missing words

Big business decisions involve financial analysis using techniques such as
.... appraisal, analysis of accounting .... or decision
.... These methods rely upon various assumptions and may generate
conflicting evidence, for instance that an investment with higher profitability may
have a longer .... period. Therefore the final decision may rely on far
more than bare statistics.

Directors are paid to make judgements based on their experience, their market
understanding and their overall objectives. Qualitative factors often prove the
deciding ones when decisions are made.

B Which factor relates to which technique?

Write down the letter(s) corresponding to the factor(s) that relate to each of the listed
techniques. Each letter can be used more than once.

1 Investment appraisal ....   2 Decision trees   ....

3 Ratio analysis   ....   4 Correlation   ....

5 Sales forecasting   ....

a) Company objectives may override numerical factors

b) It may be impossible to be sure of cause and effect

c) Data is based on historic evidence – may now be out of date

d) Probabilities may be too subject to inaccuracy or bias

e) Human factors such as morale are unquantifiable, but still important

f) May be based on extrapolation, assuming future will be like the past

g) The technique ignores uncertainty and risk

h) The technique ignores possible impacts upon corporate image

i) May not compare like with like, e.g. accounting differences between firms

j) Hinges on the accuracy of cash flow forecasts over several years

C Data response

JK Co., a small producer of chemicals, must choose between two investments

(a) a £120,000 air filtration system that will protect staff and local residents from fumes, and save the firm from substantial fines

(b) a £150,000 packing robot that will save £75,000 of labour costs per year

JK Co.'s Finance Director has produced a quantitative appraisal that shows

	Investment (a)	Investment (b)
Pay-back period	3.75 years	2 years
Average rate of return	14.5%	19.75%
Net Present Value (of DCF)	+£52,000	+£105,000

1 If you were JK Co.'s personnel manager, outline two arguments you might use to press for Investment (a).

2 The Finance Director is known to be keen on automation. How may this have influenced the investment appraisal results he has produced?

3 The Managing Director is very keen to improve JK Co.'s image among local residents and staff, but is answerable to quite active shareholders. Identify two reasons for, and two against, deciding on Investment (b).

Examiners' Notes

In financial decisions as in all decisions, judgement is the most crucial influence on success or failure. Judging the risks v. the rewards, the effects of a decision upon staff, customers or other stakeholders and the influence upon meeting business objectives. Never underestimate qualitative issues, because examiners love to set up situations where they outweigh quantitative factors.

Quality management

A Missing words

Traditionally, 'quality' meant quality .... , i.e. inspectors at the end of a production line making sure that defective items did not get through to the public. Then came a move to quality assurance, which ensured that production systems were so well monitored and regulated that quality consistency was virtually guaranteed. Most powerfully of all, TQM (T...................... Q........................... M....................................) swept Britain in the early 1990s. It aimed to change the workplace culture, establishing the primary need for quality in all tasks and at all times.

Whereas in the days of quality inspection, achieving quality was thought of as a cost, TQM was supported by the idea that getting things 'right .... time' would cut costs and wastage.

B Tick the relevant category for each of these factors

	Quality Control	Quality Assurance	TQM
1 Efficient measurement of quality standards			
2 System for rectifying defects at end of the line			
3 Quality auditors check systems every year or two			
4 All staff sent on quality training courses			
5 Customer satisfaction a key part of every decision			

C State which terms have the following definitions

1 A British system for providing quality assurance certification. ....

2 Measuring your own quality levels against the best in your industry. ....

3 When individual employees measure their own quality levels. ....

4 Achieving continuous improvement (in quality levels). ....

D Data response

Look at this quality data for three producers of bicycles, then answer the questions below.

	Rally	Drake	Mountain
% of material scrapped	6.5	12	7.5
% of work 'right first time'	79	47	86
Customer complaints per 1000 bikes	54	23	18
% of customers delighted with their bike	23	8	31
% of work rejected at final inspection	n/a	22	3.5

1 Which of the three producers has each of the following quality policies? Briefly explain your answers.

a) Quality control

....

....

b) TQM

....

....

c) Quality assurance

....

....

2 State three possible consequences for Mountain of having achieved the highest result for 'customer delight'.

....

....

3 State three possible costs of boosting quality standards.

....

....

Examiners' Notes

Success in managing quality is the key to customer satisfaction, repeat purchasing, the consumer image of the business and the self respect shown (or not shown) by staff. Never make it sound easy to achieve, or something you can take for granted.

Ratios

A Missing words

Ratios are a way of interpreting published .... by comparing one figure to another. Then the company's performance can be judged against the previous .... , in relation to its rivals, or compared with accountants' norms, such as that the acid test should be around .... This enables analysts to quickly pick key information out of the mass of figures within a company's annual report.

B Good or bad?

You judge, then briefly comment.

1 A fishmonger has a stock turnover of 12.

....

2 A sandwich bar's debtor days figure is 30.

....

3 A rapidly growing, profitable firm has a gearing level of 60%.

....

....

4 An engineering firm's return on capital is 16.3%.

....

....

C Jot down two ways a firm could

1 Reduce gearing.

....

....

2 Boost its liquidity position.

....

....

3 Boost its asset turnover.

....

....

....

4 Reduce debtor days.

....

....

D *Cause and effect*

Put in an arrow to indicate the direction from cause to effect. Is the cause one-way or two-way? If one way, which way? See the example given in 1.

1 Falling profit margins	⟵	Falling sales
2 Lower gearing	....	Rising asset turnover
3 Rising profits	....	Rising asset turnover
4 Falling stock turnover	....	Falling sales
5 Cut in stock levels	....	Rise in acid test ratio

E *Anagrams*

1 The scent of profit	RING OF ARMPITS	....
2 More debt than equity	GIN RAGE	....
3 Make them sweat	VAST NORSE, TRUE	....
4 Nice and liquid?	CAT SITED	....

Examiners' Notes

Useful though ratios may be, never forget that by the time they are published, ratios may no longer show the true picture; remember also that they can be window-dressed; ratios raise questions, they do not answer them.

Recruitment, induction and training

A Missing words

Some firms leave recruitment to quite junior people in the Human
.... Management department. Others devote a huge amount of
time, effort and senior staff to the task of finding and attracting the best possible
staff. Bill Gates of M... , for example, makes a point of meeting
all new graduate recruits to his software empire.

Top organisations know they need top people at every level. Then they must provide
top quality .... training to help the new recruits settle in. For
graduate recruits, a year or two of on-the-job .... might consist
of spending six months at each of the firm's key departments.

B Match the practice to the leadership style

For each leadership style write down the letter(s) corresponding to the recruitment
practice and training approach(es) likely to be used.

1 Laissez-faire ....   2 Democratic ....

3 Paternalistic ....   4 Authoritarian ....

Recruitment practice	Training approach
a) Interview focus upon sporting and social activities	w) Training focused solely on acquiring new skills required in the workplace
b) Psychometric testing of attitudes and compliance	x) Training may be for team-building or career-building (such as public speaking)
c) Careful use of CV, references and interview focusing on ambitions and abilities	y) Little or no training offered; thought better to learn by doing
d) Brief interview to ensure that the recruit is 'the right sort of person'	z) Provide training wanted by the individual, e.g. a language or a management course; focus on the person, not the firm

C True or False?

Place a T or an F by each of the following statements.

1 Research shows that most interviewers make their mind up about a candidate within a few seconds. ☐

2 Psychometric tests are designed to catch out those who are not being truthful. ☐

3 Induction is limited to the training that takes place on the first day of a new job. ☐

4 Large firms may spend more than £20,000 per candidate when recruiting new graduate trainees. ☐

D Data response

When Stan Martin went for an interview at the Ministry of Defence, he was surprised to be interviewed by a Personnel Officer, not a line manager. The interview went superbly, as both shared a devotion to the band *Marillion*.

Stan's first day in the accounts department was a bit of a shock, as his boss was a very dull, middle-aged woman who was clearly bored with the work. By the end of the day, Stan knew he would learn little from her. Fortunately, colleagues in the department seemed friendly, as all felt the same dislike of their boss.

1 State one reason in favour of, and one against, job interviews being conducted by the line manager (not the personnel/human resources department).

....

....

2 From a firm's point of view, why is it important that a new recruit should know exactly what to expect in a job, however bad?

....

....

3 Give two reasons why off-the-job training may be helpful to Stan.

....

....

Remuneration

A Missing words

Remuneration means every type of financial reward received by someone who works (including managers, workers and business owners).

> Workers may receive little more than their pay, plus holiday pay plus sick pay. Managers often have these, plus employer pension contributions, plus company car and possibly private health care (these are known as .... benefits).
>
> The key issues about remuneration are:
>
> - do workers and managers have different terms and conditions or is there .... status?
>
> - are staff paid by time (hourly rate or salary) or by the amount they have produced, e.g. .... -work.
>
> Motivation theorists such as .... believed financial incentives to be crucial, whereas .... believed money was not a motivator.

B Which term is defined by each of the following?

1 An annual supplement given in addition to salary, to reflect an employee's achievements in relation to agreed goals. ....

2 Payment per item produced. ....

3 An annual bonus paid as a percentage of the profits made by the business. ....

4 Staff remuneration in addition to pay. ....

C Explain two reasons why

1 Herzberg believed that 'the worst way to pay people is on piecework'.

....

....

....

2 High pay levels and share options given to Directors may damage a firm's long-term performance.

....

....

....

3 Giving executives company cars may be seen as socially irresponsible.

....

....

....

D Match the payment method to the relevant advantage and disadvantage

1 Piecework ....

2 Performance-related pay ....

3 Profit sharing ....

4 Employee share ownership ....

5 Straight salary ....

Advantage	Disadvantage
a) May encourage cost cutting	**v)** Some staff may become complacent and under-achieve
b) Can focus on the job itself	**w)** Reinforces behaviour, encouraging resistance to change
c) Encourages high output levels	**x)** May cause incentive problems during a bear market
d) Encourages effort to achieve a range of goals at work	**y)** A risk of favouritism and that few will risk criticising or arguing
e) May lead to long-term outlook	**z)** Individuals may not see their efforts affecting company profit

Examiners' **Notes**

Above all else, remember this term! When exams ask about remuneration, many answers are left blank because students' minds have gone blank. Make it one of your 'night before' check points.

Research & Development

A Missing words

R&D means scientific .... and technical ....
This is directed at creating or improving products, rather than finding out what the consumer wants and thinks. The latter information is the function of market

....

For businesses, the ideal is a combination of good market research and good R&D.

Students often undermine a passage of analysis by using the terms interchangeably.

B Draw arrows to match the issue to the consequence

Important issue regarding R&D	Potential consequence of the issue
1 How can managers measure whether today's spending on R&D will ever pay off?	**a)** May reduce R&D spending, as all this year's costs are charged to this year's Profit and Loss Account
2 It's treated in Britain as revenue expenditure, but isn't it an investment in the future, like capital expenditure?	**b)** Adds value, reduces price elasticity and can be a major source of competitive advantage nationally and internationally
3 Successful R&D can lead to highly differentiated, or even unique, patented products	**c)** It's always tempting to cut back budgets for 'inessentials', especially in recessions
4 Timescales and company objectives (R&D usually takes 5–12 years to pay off, if at all)	**d)** Firms find it hard to continue funding R&D unless there's a clear commercial result
5 Britain has traditionally been good at inventions (research), but Japan, far better at getting them to market (development)	**e)** Short-termist firms will never have the patience to invest in this way

C R&D or market research?

For each of the following, write down whether it is an example of R&D or MR (market research).

1 Sunny Delight was launched after two years of test marketing in Carlisle, to find out its sales potential. ....

2 JVC developed and patented the VHS recording system. Since then they
   have earned over £100 million in royalty payments from other electronics
   firms.   ....

3 Glaxo's discovery and development of the anti-ulcer drug Zantac led to
   sales of over £10,000 million during the 20-year life of its patent.   ....

4 In blind product tests, Cadbury's found that many young people
   preferred the taste of Galaxy.   ....

D Explain why

1 A strong R&D section is vital for a firm operating in a market with short product life
   cycles.

2 Good design can boost profits hugely.

E Which of the following factors are the keys to stimulating demand for these products?

Write down the letters corresponding to up to three factors per brand.

Product/brand	Demand stimulus
1 A Mercedes open-top sports car	a) Price
2 A Manchester United training top	b) Quality of design
3 A Gucci watch	c) Quality of manufacture
4 A Boeing 747 jet aircraft (price; £110 million)	d) Innovative R&D
5 A Sony Playstation 2	e) Extensive TV advertising
6 A box of Mars Celebrations	f) Special promotional offer

Examiners' Notes

Examiners love to test whether you can distinguish between R&D and market research. Remember that R&D is scientific (not market) research and technical development. It's about the product, not the customers.

Safety margin

A Missing words

Few businesses can predict their futures with accuracy; price wars break out, recessions arrive and fashion may turn against your product. Therefore it is not enough to measure current .... (revenue − costs); it is also wise to check the .... margin. This shows the amount by which sales can fall before the firm starts making losses. This is usually measured in terms of sales volume, but it is also very helpful to look at it in percentage terms.

Formulae:

1. Safety margin (in units) = Sales volume − Break-even point (in units)

2. Percentage safety margin = $\dfrac{\text{Sales volume} - \text{Break-even point}}{\text{Sales volume}} \times 100$

B Elementary calculations

1 A firm with sales of 50,000 units breaks even at 30,000. Calculate its safety margin

   a) by volume, and

   ....

   b) as a percentage of sales.

   ....

2 Rufus Ltd has a sales revenue of £400,000 per month and a break-even point of 70,000 units. Its average selling price is £4.

   Calculate the safety margin by volume and by value.

   ....

   ....

3 Brevity plc has sales of 12,000 units per week at £20 each, variable costs of £12 per unit and weekly fixed costs of £80,000.

   Calculate

   a) its break-even point, and

   ....

   ....

b) its safety margin.

....

....

C Draw arrows to match the use to the formula

Practical use	Formula
1 To show safety margin by value	**a)** Sales volume − Break-even point
2 To show the sales needed for a loss-maker to reach break-even	**b)** Sales revenue − Break-even revenue
3 To show the amount sales can decline before losses are made	**c)** Break-even point − Sales volume

D Harder calculations

1 A Chief Executive is worried that his firm's safety margin of 1,000 units is only 10% of sales. Contribution per unit is £2.

Calculate

a) break-even output ....

b) fixed costs ....

c) profit ....

2 A firm with sales of £60,000 per month has a £2 selling price, contribution per unit of £1.20 and monthly fixed costs of £30,000.

Calculate

a) the break-even point ....

b) the safety margin ....

c) the monthly profit ....

E Explain two

1 Reasons why it is useful to look at safety margin as a percentage of sales.

....

....

2 Ways a firm could act to increase its safety margin.

....

Secondary research

A Missing words

Secondary research looks for data that has already been gathered, perhaps by government or by commercial research organisations.

It is a good source of background information on markets such as market .... (by volume or value), the market .... of the main businesses within the industry and underlying trends, such as that sales are rising by 5–10% a year. After carrying out this process (also called d.......................... research), firms can identify what remaining, tailor-made information they need to gather through .... research.

B Draw arrows to match the need to the source

Source	Need
1 Government statistics	a) Market size and trends
2 Retail audits	b) Economic growth figures for China
3 Market intelligence reports, e.g. Mintel	c) Latest sales figures for Tesco
4 Trade or business press	d) Population trend data for 9–15 year olds
5 Company annual reports	e) Latest shop sales figures for different brands of vodka

C Fill in the gaps

1 Before entering a new market, the first thing to find out is the market .... and growth, so that provisional costings and sales forecasts can be made.

2 A business faced with a sharp downturn in its sales should gather secondary data on market .... to find out whether it has lost market .... or whether its rivals are struggling equally.

3 Retail .... allow a manufacturer to anticipate changes in factory demand, as today's ups and downs in retail demand become tomorrow's changes in orders.

4 .... data enables a firm such as Mothercare to anticipate broad changes in demand, e.g. the need to open more stores if the birth rate is increasing.

D Explain two

1 Reasons why small firms should make use of secondary data.

....

....

2 Disadvantages of using secondary data such as Mintel reports.

....

....

3 Reasons why secondary data should be treated with caution.

....

....

Examiners' Notes

Second-hand, but not second-rate. What could be more valuable than knowing the market growth rate, and therefore whether your firm's growth is good or bad? Students tend to underestimate secondary research.

Shareholders' ratios

A Missing words

Well-informed shareholders are interested in many aspects of a firm's accounts. They will want to look at the .... ratio, to find if the firm is over-borrowed and the .... test ratio to examine its liquidity position. Most important of all, they will be interested in its profits, probably in relation to the capital employed in the business (the ROC).

Yet why do people invest in equity (......................) capital?

Partly because they hope for capital gains, if the share price rises, and partly because of the annual income they can receive from the .... declared from the company's profits. For example, at the time of writing, shares in Iceland Frozen Foods pay an annual dividend worth 4.5% of the sum invested. This is slightly more than most banks offer on savings accounts, so Iceland shareholders have a reasonable annual income plus the chance of making a capital profit.

B Explain why

1 A firm might go on paying dividends, even when going through a loss-making period.

....

....

2 The dividend yield on a share may be more useful to a share buyer than the dividend per share.

....

....

3 It would be risky to rely for income on a share with a very high dividend yield.

....

....

C Calculations

1 A firm has an issued share capital of 200,000 £1 shares and it declares an annual dividend of £60,000.

Calculate

a) the dividend per share

....

b) the dividend yield, assuming the shares are currently trading at £5 each.

....

2 An investor buys 5,000 25p shares at a market price of £1.20 each. Later in the year the company declares a dividend of £60,000 on its 1,000,000 issued ordinary shares.

Calculate

a) dividend per share

....

....

b) dividend yield

....

....

c) the dividend cheque the shareholder will receive.

....

D Data response

	£000
Sales turnover	1,650
Gross profit	965
Overheads	725
Trading profit	240
One-off items	605
Pre-tax profit	845
Corporation tax	185
Profit after tax	660
Dividends	260

1 What is the company's retained profit?

....

....

2 Do you think the firm was right to declare a dividend of £260,000? Explain your reasoning.

....

....

....

....

....

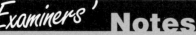

Examiners' Notes

Everyone finds these shareholder ratios tough. The key one is dividend yield; remember to compare it with the interest rate, but never forget that firms can cut their dividends, so the yield is never guaranteed.

Social constraints

A Missing words

Businesses such as Shell, Esso and Barclays have experienced difficult periods as a result of failing to manage effectively their external relations. For Shell and Esso, environmental and ethical issues led to periods of threatened consumer boycott and awkward questioning of the C........................ at the shareholders' annual g........................ meeting.

Firms need to respond to changing social or political pressures, though within limits. Some multinational firms have been guilty of working too closely with dictatorships in Africa and South East Asia. The culture of a well-run business should clarify the dividing line between what is and is not morally acceptable.

B Identify the terms defined below, then give the word formed by taking the first letter of each

1 The costs borne by society as a result of a business decision or action.

   ....

2 A social .... is an independent account of aspects of business such as staff health and consumer safety.

3 When the interaction of supply and demand fails to provide the most efficient outcome.

   ....

4 An organisation formed to campaign for an issue such as banning the testing of chemical products on animals.

   ....

5 Putting pressure on influential people such as Members of Parliament, to try to affect decisions.

   ....

6 The values and principles that may enable business people to do what is morally right, even if it hits profit.

   ....

   Answer ....

C Do you agree or disagree?

Write an A (agree) or D (disagree) in the box, then briefly explain your reasoning.

1 It was unethical for Virgin to exploit its London to Manchester railway monopoly by increasing fares by 80% in three years. ☐

   ....

   ....

2 A firm is being ethical if its marketing strategy focuses on the healthy aspects of its hamburgers. ☐

   ....

3 Firms with autocratic leadership may be more ethical, as the moral responsibility for decisions rests clearly with one person. ☐

....

....

D Explain why

1 Oil companies such as BP and Shell were among the first to carry out annual environmental audits.

....

....

2 Firms with well-known company or brand names use contingency planning with care.

....

....

....

3 Direct action has become more important than parliamentary lobbying these days.

....

....

E Opportunities or threats?

Put an O (opportunity), a T (threat) or both by each of the following.

1 Economic growth in low-cost China is forecast to average 10% a year for the next three years. ....

2 The government brings in a new law that every plc should carry out and publish an annual social audit. ....

3 A firm is offered a huge, highly profitable contract on condition that a 10% 'commission' is paid. ....

4 A new government promises to scrap all laws affecting business, 'to abolish red tape'. ....

5 Due to skill shortages, a firm cuts its electricians' training programme to finance hiring experienced staff. ....

6 Posters appear at your factory entrance, put up by those protesting at your use of animal furs to make coats. ....

7 As a restaurateur, you are interested to note the increasing interest in organic food and drink. ....

8 The earth proves to warm up faster than predicted, causing heat waves and droughts in British summers. ....

Social responsibilities

A Missing words

Businesses tackle social responsibilities for one or more of three reasons: legal requirements, self-interest or moral conviction.

> Some firms consider their responsibilities in relation to their .... (groups with an interest in the firm's success or failure), others take an even wider view, perhaps sponsoring educational initiatives that offer no obvious pay-back. However, many public .... companies focus so much on shareholders/profit, that it is hard to see much substance to their claims to be socially responsible.

B Why do they do it?

Identify the possible reason or reasons for each of the following, by jotting down an L for legal requirement, an S for self-interest or an M for moral conviction (there may be more than one answer).

1 Equal pay for equal work. ....

2 Providing company cars. ....

3 Providing safe working conditions. ....

4 Zero pollution from the factory. ....

5 Paying for staff on degree courses. ....

6 Ensuring high quality products. ....

7 Using organic ingredients. ....

8 Providing equal opportunities. ....

9 Running a 'computers for schools' promotion. ....

10 Advertising the company's commitment to the environment. ....

11 Selling products that do what they say they will do. ....

12 Refusing to collude with 'rivals' to fix prices. ....

C Give two reasons why

1 Looking after staff is in a firm's best interest.

....

....

2   A small firm might take short cuts over customer safety.

....

....

3   Managers might focus on shareholders/profit far more than their other stakeholders.

....

....

4   Firms with strong brand names are likely to act responsibly.

....

....

D *Which social responsibility was ignored in each of the following situations?*

1   An oil company disposing of an oil rig by sinking it in the North Sea.

....

2   A car producer failing to spend the $11 per car needed to stop faulty petrol tanks causing fatal car fires.

....

3   A major insurance company whose sales staff persuaded customers to buy inappropriate pension plans.

....

E *Social responsibility or marketing strategy?*

Briefly state which you think apply to the following, and why.

1   The Co-op Bank promising that they will not lend to arms manufacturers.

....

2   Coca-Cola sponsoring the Olympics.

....

....

3   Body Shop using social and environmental audits.

....

....

4   A bank producing free teaching materials on money management.

....

....

Sources of finance

A Missing words

Most companies raise most of their finance from within their own resources, i.e. .... finance such as trading profit. About 60% of all finance for expansion comes from this source.

Sometimes, though, there are such attractive growth opportunities that managers are unwilling to wait for internal finance to accumulate. Therefore .... sources are approached, such as loans or equity, i.e. .... capital. Injections of capital from outside have financed many of Virgin's new projects, such as Virgin Trains.

B Internal or external sources?

Put the following into the right column.

bank loans   venture capital   asset sales   share capital   profit

debenture   squeezing working capital   cutting costs

Internal sources of capital	External sources of capital
1	1
2	2
3	3
4	4

C Explain two

1 Disadvantages of using an overdraft as a source of long-term finance.

    ....

    ....

2 Reasons why business owners may be reluctant to float onto the stock exchange.

    ....

    ....

3 Reasons why trading profit is ideal for financing expansion.

....

....

D Match the source to the need

Identify two sources for each of the requirements **1–5**.

1 To cover trading losses during a recession.   ....

2 For replacing 1,000 computers on an aging network.   ....

3 To finance a major expansion overseas.   ....

4 To finance rapid sales increases for a small firm.   ....

5 To finance the purchase of an office block.   ....

a) Overdraft	**v)** Reinvested profit
b) 2–5 year bank loan	**w)** 25-year debenture
c) Rights issue to raise extra share capital	**x)** Extended credit from supplier
d) Credit factoring	**y)** Venture capital
e) Sale and leaseback	**z)** Selling under-used fixed assets

Examiners' Notes

Remember that 60% of finance for new investment comes from reinvested profit. Students are too quick to suggest loans or share capital. These are last resorts. Firms begin by seeing how to finance their ambitions through internal sources. The type of finance must be appropriate to its use; for instance, a short-term, seasonal dip in cash flow can be met by an overdraft, whereas a debenture is better suited to financing the purchase of freehold property.

Special order decisions

A Missing words

Special order decisions arise when there is an opportunity to sell extra output to a new or an existing customer. It will often be at a .... price than is usually charged.

However complex the question or the numbers seem, the key to tackling special order decisions is to focus upon the net contribution generated, i.e. .... from the order minus any extra fixed costs incurred. In other words, a special order decision should be made on the basis of the marginal .... and costs from accepting it.

B Calculations

1 Fodan Ltd has sales of 2,000 units a month at £10 per unit. Unit variable costs are £4 and the monthly fixed overheads come to £9,000.

a) What is its current monthly profit? ....

b) A new customer has just offered to buy 600 units at £7 each. If Fodan Ltd accepts, what effect will it have on the coming month's profit?

   ....

2 The Tigana Wine Co. sells 800 bottles a week at £5 each. Its weekly fixed costs are £1,200, variable costs are £2.50 per unit and average costs per unit are £4. When the buyer from Tesco offers to buy an extra 600 bottles per week at £3.20 each, Tigana is furious.

   'How can they expect me to sell at 80p below cost?'

   It takes his assistant, Monsieur Damiano, a little while to explain that the Tesco offer will boost weekly profit by more than 50%.

a) Calculate the profit made by the Tigana Wine Co. before and after the special order from Tesco.

   ....

   ....

   ....

   ....

b) Briefly explain to Tigana why his view is incorrect.

....

....

....

C Other factors to consider – true or false?

Place a T or an F by each of the following statements.

1 No special order decision should be made without checking that there is spare capacity. ☐

2 A firm with a weak cash flow position might struggle to supply an extra order. ☐

3 Special order decisions hinge on average costs versus average selling prices. ☐

4 A key issue is whether existing customers will find out about the special price you've charged. ☐

D Data response

Bristle Ltd sells horse brushes throughout Europe. Its capacity is 8,000 per month, though sales are currently 6,000, and rising. It sells mainly through small, specialist shops and directly to stables. This month's financial data shows

Revenue	£24,000
Materials	£6,000
Piece-rate labour	£9,000
Fixed overheads	£6,000

Now a buyer from Egypt has offered to buy 1,500 units a month for £3 per unit. This will be contracted for two years and will result in £5,000 of set-up costs for Bristle Ltd.

1 Calculate the profit or loss Bristle Ltd would make from this special order.

....

....

....

2 Outline four other factors the business should consider before agreeing to the order.

....

....

....

Stakeholders

A Missing words

Stakeholders are individuals or groups with an interest in the actions, successes and failures of an organisation. They include the owners (in an unlimited .... business), the .... (in a limited company), staff, suppliers, customers and local residents.

Some writers suggest that modern firms take care to respect all their stakeholders, whereas others believe that firms focus upon shareholders rather than the wider interests of all their ....

Current company law says that Directors' primary responsibility is to their

....

B Which stakeholder group is affected most by each of the following decisions?

1 A move to a policy of JIT ordering of materials. ....

2 To adopt a strategy of delayering. ....

3 A switch in transport policy from delivering by rail to using the roads. ....

4 A decision to cut dividends by 20%. ....

C Give two reasons why

1 It might be short-sighted to focus solely upon the interests of shareholders.

....

....

2 Treating all stakeholders as equal may threaten a company's performance.

....

....

....

D Data response

Look at the following data relating to two producers of cement, then answer the questions below.

	Producer A	Producer B
Profit as a % of sales revenue (profit margin)	8.4	6.7
Staff absence for health and safety reasons (% per day)	3.5	1.6
Average credit period before paying suppliers (days)	92	64
% cement dust emissions escaping from factory	2.9	1.3

1 Which producer seems to act more responsibly towards its staff?

....

2 Which producer seems more focused upon its shareholders than its stakeholders?

....

Briefly explain your answer.

....

....

3 Why might there be a conflict of interest between stakeholders, if company A was deciding what to do about its cement dust emissions?

....

....

4 What evidence is there that producer A may be acting in a short-termist manner?

....

....

Examiners' Notes

This topic is very important for Business exams. If you feel you need to know more, read Unit 69 of *Business Studies* by Marcousé *et al.*, published by Hodder & Stoughton Educational.

Stock control

A Missing words

Controlling stock is crucial to .... costs and to
.... customer satisfaction.

Traditionally, firms set a .... stock, which is the minimum desired
stock level. New stock must be ordered early enough to ensure that it arrives before
stocks .... below this minimum level. This time period is known as the
.... time.

Nowadays, many firms adopt a JIT (J........................ I............ T........................) approach,
which attempts to operate without the safety net of a .... stock.

B Key factors in efficient stock management

Explain very briefly

1 How can stock rotation help to minimise the costs of holding stock?

   ....

2 Why do firms need higher buffer stocks when there's a long supplier lead time?

   ....

   ....

3 Why is laser scanning so helpful in keeping stock levels low?

   ....

   ....

C Data response

Look at the diagram (on the facing page) of a retailer's stocks of gloves, then answer the
questions below.

1 Between weeks one and ten, what are the weekly sales of gloves?

   ....

2 If the supplier of 'Superwarm' gloves has a lead time of 3 weeks, what reorder level
   does the retailer need to set?

   ....

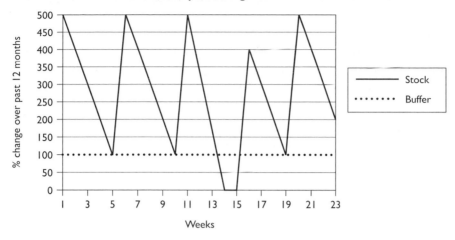

Stock of 'Superwarm' gloves

% change over past 12 months

Weeks

Stock

Buffer

3 What is the firm's desired minimum stock level? ....

4 Explain what happens to the retailer after week 10.

....

....

D *Give two reasons why*

1 Customers can be let down by a Just In Time stock control system.

....

2 Firms tend to cut stocks when interest rates are high.

....

....

3 Effective stock management can help a firm's liquidity position.

....

....

Examiners' Notes

Remember that good stock control is not only good operations management, but also vital for successful marketing (getting repeat custom in retail, for example) and for keeping costs down.

Strategic thinking

A Missing words

Strategic thinking involves analysing the underlying issues facing the business and identifying an appropriate long-term plan or solution. It involves:

i)   careful analysis of the firm's existing situation and future prospects, using techniques such as the B........................... Matrix;

ii) assessment of the external environment, i.e. factors outside the firm's control such as competition, and economic, social and institutional change (new European .... laws, for instance);

iii) assessment of the firm's resources, e.g. machines, money and

....

Having made these assessments, strategy may require bold – even harsh – decisions, such as selling off or closing down any under-performing part of the business. In 2001 Marks & Spencer closed down its overseas stores, and it did so in an apparently thoughtless manner which resulted in very bad publicity.

B Strategic thinking or not?

Say yes or no, then briefly state your reason.

1 Levi's 2000 launch of Engineered Jeans, targeted at a young, fashionable market.

....

2 Iceland Foods' 1998 decision to focus on organic foods (it withdrew from this approach in 2001).

....

....

3 BMW's sale of Rover Cars for £10 in 2000.

....

....

4 Sainsbury's use of Buy One Get One Free sales promotions in Summer 2001.

....

C Constraints on strategic thinking

Draw arrows to match the constraint to the relevant strategy.

Objective	Constraint
1 When Levi first started producing jeans outside the US	a) Major change for a business can require a wide range of extra skills and resources
2 Nintendo moving into the mobile phone market	b) Breaking through traditional management attitudes
3 BD Ltd deciding to try to build up export sales to France	c) Massive initial investment costs are a barrier to entry

D Which is the greatest strategic triumph?

Choose one of the following; explain why it's such a triumph.

1 Nokia's 1990 shift from making paper and car tyres to concentrating on the then unknown mobile phone.

2 Nintendo's 1970s shift from 100 years of making playing cards to developing electronic games.

3 Mercedes in the 1990s switching from large-cars-only to develop the small 'Smart' and 'A Class' cars.

Answer ....

....

....

....

....

Examiners' **Notes**

This means thinking long term, thinking big and thinking in a way that will probably affect the whole business. Beware of obvious thoughts, such as price promotions or other short-term gimmicks.

SWOT and strategy

A Missing words

> SWOT analysis examines the factors that are within a firm's control or influence (its S............................ and W....................................) and those that are outside its control (its O............................ and T............................).
>
> It is easy to underestimate the difficulty of identifying strengths and weaknesses. They may seem obvious to an outsider, or to an employee in one department, but who has the whole picture? In theory, senior management should know the real strengths and weaknesses of a business. Yet in 1999–2001 Sainsbury's, Marks & Spencer and Iceland were all guilty of stumbling on serious weaknesses. Was it lack of knowledge or was it a refusal to listen that led all three into serious downturns? It may be that shopfloor staff knew, but poor vertical .... kept the managers in the dark.

B S, W, O or T?

Categorise each of the following features of an independent pizza restaurant and take-away, by writing in S, W, O or T.

1 A lot of competition locally from national chains and other independents. ☐

2 Located just off a main road with little passing traffic. ☐

3 Makes high-quality pizzas from a huge, blazing wood-fired oven. ☐

4 Struggles to retain staff. ☐

5 Has a distinctive brand name and logo. ☐

6 Prices are quite high, so takings may suffer in a recession. ☐

7 Aims to open five other outlets over next 12 months, though in better locations. ☐

8 Takings on Thursday to Sunday evenings are good, but trade at lunchtimes has not been developed. ☐

9 Menu is targeted at adults, with little for their children; yet the local residents are mainly families. ☐

10 Home delivery accounts for 35% of takings; was originally budgeted at 60%. ☐

C State whether each of the following is a strategic or a tactical decision

1 To focus the energies and resources of the business upon its strengths (not correcting weaknesses). ....

2 To tackle sales weakness in the North-East with a major sales promotion based on Buy One Get One Free. ....

3 To address a potential sales threat from an Italian firm by launching a complete range of Italian products. ....

4 To seize the opportunity to open the first chain of luxury ice cream outlets in China. ....

D Data response

On Sarah's first day she was introduced to Brian, Chief Executive of Bristow Software. She asked if the business had a SWOT analysis she could read. The answer was no, but Brian agreed to spend half an hour answering questions.

Sarah found that the strengths Brian mentioned could all be categorised as marketing or finance. The weaknesses were mainly to do with people and operations. She pointed this out, but Brian seemed just to accept this as a fact of life. When it came to opportunities, Brian talked with huge enthusiasm about a new, web-based software product. An hour later, when it came to asking about threats Brian announced that he had to prepare for another meeting.

1 Give two reasons why firms might benefit from preparing a written SWOT analysis annually.

....

....

2 Suggest two reasons implied in the text about the limitations of a written SWOT for a firm such as Bristow.

....

....

3 Identifying threats implies the need for contingency planning. Why might Brian be reluctant to do this?

....

....

Examiners' Notes

Analysing strengths and weaknesses is vital, but beware of overstating the ease with which a business can solve its problems. Strategy offers no magic cures for firms such as Marks & Spencer.

Takeovers

A Missing words

1 A takeover .... occurs when two or more firms are bidding for the same company.

2 When deciding on a price to bid, firms take into account tangible and .... assets.

3 Ultimately, the success or failure of a takeover bid lies in the hands of the ....

B Types of takeover

Below are listed four mergers/takeovers that have taken place in recent years. For each one, decide whether the integration was: horizontal, backward vertical, forward vertical or conglomerate.

1 WHSmith, book retailer, bought Hodder & Stoughton, a book publisher.

2 The American superstore and supermarket chain Wal-Mart, bought Asda.

3 British transport company Stagecoach bought an American operator of school buses.

4 Granada (TV and hotels) bought Letts Revise Guides.

C Identify the following terms relating to takeovers

1 An agreement between two firms of similar size to pool management and ownership.

2 A takeover bid made despite opposition from the defending company's management.

3 The premium the buyer is prepared to pay for a company's intangible assets.

D Explain the meaning of these takeover terms

1 White knight ....

....

2 Synergy ....

E Takeovers and balance sheets

Trussocks plc is bidding £4 million for Hassocks plc.

	Trussocks plc (£000s)	Hassocks plc (£000s)
Fixed assets	8,200	1,600
Stock	1,600	700
Debtors and cash	2,800	300
Current liabilities	2,900	1,000
Net current assets	1,500	0
ASSETS EMPLOYED	9,700	2,600
Loans	3,200	1,300
Share capital	400	500
Reserves	6,100	800
CAPITAL EMPLOYED	9,700	2,600

Look at the balance sheets of both firms, then decide whether the statements below are true or false. (You will need a calculator.)

1 Hassocks' acid test ratio is 1.0, which shows its liquidity is fine.

2 Hassocks' gearing is 50%, which is quite high.

3 Trussocks is valuing the goodwill of Hassocks at £2.7 million.

4 If Hassocks' share capital is made up of 10p shares, the bid is worth £8 per share.

Examiners' Notes

Are takeovers carried out for logical business reasons such as economies of scale? Or for a combination of self-delusion (I'm a great manager so I can run that business better than the current Board) and self-promotion (I want a bigger empire)? Have you a view? If not, why not?

Time-based management

A Missing words

Economists suggest that there are three key resources: land, labour and capital. Businesses value a further resource equally highly: ....

This is partly because today's consumer places a huge premium on convenience and speed (hence ready-to-cook meals, 'fast food' and 1 hour photo-processing). It is also because getting a new idea to market .... can provide a huge commercial benefit; the so-called, first-mover advantage.

B Which terms are defined by the following?

1 Carrying out design and engineering development work at the same time, instead of one following the other.   ....

2 The time between receiving an order and delivering it.   ....

3 The benefit from beating your rivals to the market with a new product idea.   ....

4 Ordering supplies so that they arrive exactly when needed, i.e. with no buffer stock.   ....

C Causes and effects

Some of the following statements are causes and some are effects of being first to the market with a new product or service. Write a C or an E by each cause and effect. Put an N by any that are neither.

1 Can secure an image as 'the original'.   ☐

2 Can skim the market.   ☐

3 Simultaneous engineering.   ☐

4 High levels of retail distribution.   ☐

5 Good links between R&D and market research.   ☐

6 Good project management team.   ☐

7 Benefits from public relations 'hype' at launch.   ☐

8 Bold, swift decision making.   ☐

D *Briefly state two benefits to a business of*

1 Cutting customer lead times

....

....

2 Cutting supplier lead times

....

....

3 Simultaneous engineering

....

....

4 Just In Time stock ordering

....

....

E *Time-based drawbacks*

Put a D by disadvantages of time-based management.

1 Risks rushed decisions based on little evidence. ☐

2 Risk of over-stocking due to bulk buying. ☐

3 Risk that quality may be sacrificed to speed. ☐

4 Focus on time may mean too little focus on costs. ☐

5 Better to get it right than to get in first. ☐

6 Today's consumers are more relaxed about time. ☐

Examiners' **Notes**

Take care to separate time-based management from lean production; they are related but not identical. Lean production tries to eliminate all types of waste; time-based management focuses upon just one resource: time.

Trade unions

A Missing words

Trade unions are membership organisations that represent the interests of
.... in the workplace. To belong, you must pay a fee that might
amount to £10–£15 per month.

Although traditionally the most important role of a union was to negotiate on pay
and conditions for all members (........................ bargaining), these days unions spend
most of their time and resources helping members with individual problems, such as
discrimination at work. A union can provide expert advice on the legal position of
staff and, if necessary, hire a .... to pursue a case. Few individuals
could afford legal advice, therefore union membership can be seen as an insurance
policy against unfair treatment at work.

B Draw arrows to match the problem to the union response

Problem	Response
1 Ambulance drivers' pay has slipped behind the rate of inflation for two years	a) Organise a lobbying campaign locally, and threaten strike action from staff at the firm's other factories
2 A pregnant employee with just 3 months at the firm is unsure of her right to paid leave	b) Check whether the individual matches the firm's stated procedures for selecting staff (e.g. first in first out)
3 A young Asian shop steward has been selected for redundancy	c) Negotiate hard within the usual collective bargaining process, but also push for media support
4 At a bank, 58% of junior staff are women, but only 13% of senior staff	d) Send a copy of the precise regulations, plus the union's own guide setting out the main points
5 A large car firm has announced the closure of its factory in Coventry, with 3,000 job losses	e) The union may take the evidence to the Equal Opportunities Commission to discuss possible legal action

C *Identify the following definitions, then find the word formed by the first letter of each*

1 Drawing a clear dividing line between one job function and another – the opposite of multiskilling.

....

2 When an employer accepts the right of a union to represent staff within a workplace.

....

3 When an independent person is brought in to judge the appropriate solution to an industrial dispute.

....

4 Industrial action in which staff work to the letter of their employment contracts.

....

Answer ....

D *Explain two possible*

1 Advantages to a company of recognising a trade union.

....
....

2 Disadvantages to an employee of belonging to a union.

....
....

E *Circle the odd one out in each row*

1 Arbitration   Conciliation   Delegation

2 Work to rule   Demarcation   Overtime ban

3 Increase job security   Increase pay   Increase labour turnover

Examiners' Notes

Do not treat unions as if their role is to 'make trouble'; their objective is to further the interests of their members. Firms such as Tesco are clear that unions can help management gain a fuller understanding of staff needs and motivations.

Unemployment

A Missing words

Businesses affect and are affected by unemployment.

> When it rises sharply, as in a r............................ , firms may suffer falls in demand but benefit from falling labour t............................ and reductions in wage-push pressure. Unemployment that results from an economic downturn is known as .... More long-lasting can be .... unemployment, which results from changes in demand and output that leave some employees with the wrong skills to match the jobs newly available.

B Pros and cons to business

Identify whether points **1–8** are pros or cons of cyclical unemployment (cyc) or structural unemployment (struc), e.g. **1** = pro/struc.

1 Available labour cannot be used without training.   .... / ....

2 Likely to cut demand for luxuries within certain regions.   .... / ....

3 Provides an ideal time to restructure your workforce nationally.   .... / ....

4 May be pools of available labour in certain regions or industrial sectors.   .... / ....

5 May require a new marketing strategy based on value for money.   .... / ....

6 Opportunity to open factory on a greenfield site with good supply of labour.   .... / ....

7 Should reduce voluntary labour turnover for all employers.   .... / ....

8 National demand boost for goods with negative income elasticity.   .... / ....

C Explain two probable effects of high unemployment on

1 Business costs.

....

....

2 A firm's marketing strategy.

....

....

3 Human resource management.

....

....

D Impact of high unemployment on revenue

For each of the businesses listed, put a tick in the box that shows the impact high employment would have on its revenue.

	Sharply worsen trade	Trade may fall slightly	Little or no effect	Should make business boom
1 A small bakery supplying shops, schools and hospitals				
2 A firm selling products with income elasticity of −2.5				
3 Luxury sports car manufacturer Jensen				
4 Next clothing store				

Window dressing

A Missing words

Window dressing means preparing for the end of the financial year by taking actions that present a more rosy view of a firm's financial position.

This is legal, but can be deceptive and therefore against the best interests of .... (the owners of the company). A poor .... position could be masked by selling a fixed asset for cash before the balance sheet date. Even more misleading is to deliver and invoice customers early, so that future sales revenues are recorded earlier (bringing some of next year's sales forward into this financial year). This boosts short-term revenue and profit, but at the cost of future disappointments.

B Cause and effect

What might be the reason for using the following types of window dressing, and what might be the consequence? Write in the appropriate letter(s) from the list below.

1 Conducting a sale and leaseback deal just before the balance sheet date. ....

2 Introducing brand name valuations to the balance sheet. ....

3 Failing to write-down debtor items even though there seems little chance of being paid. ....

4 Hiding effective debt levels by leasing all fixed assets. ....

Cause	Effect
a) To increase assets employed and lower the gearing ratio	w) Masks the risks of the firm's finances from creditors
b) To keep gearing levels to the minimum	x) Profit may look OK temporarily, but cash flow will be weak
c) To mask a deteriorating liquidity position	y) Creates a risk that if fashion changes, the firm's asset valuation may have to be written down
d) To avoid denting profits and the apparent liquidity position	z) A one-off injection of cash to boost the acid test ratio

C True or false?

Put a T or an F by each of these statements.

1 Deliberate window dressing is illegal in Britain.

2 When JD Co. added a £20 million brand valuation to its accounts, this boosted its cash position.

3 In 2000, a UK dot.com company exaggerated its revenue growth rate by counting 'orders' worth hundreds of thousands from its owner. This was to boost the firm's 'value' before it floated on the stock market.

4 In the 1990s, shares in the DIY firm *Wickes* collapsed when it was found that it had been overstating profits for some years by window dressing.

D Data response

Look carefully at the following data, then answer the questions below.

Chelster Football plc was under pressure from the City and was coming to the end of a dismal financial year. Last year the acid test ratio was 1.4 but, with a month to go to the end-of-year, it was heading for 0.4. To avoid the risk of a collapse of confidence in the business the Finance Director arranged a sale and leaseback on the club's training ground. This brought in enough cash to make it look as if the club's liquidity position was stable.

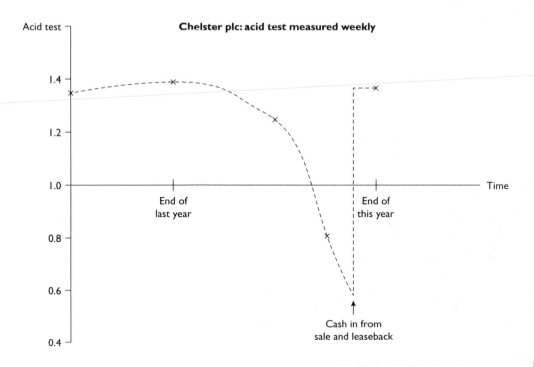

1   Identify two possible benefits to Chelster of conducting this window dressing.

    ....

    ....

2   Explain why outsiders such as creditors and shareholders would only be aware of the liquidity position as at the two end-of-year dates.

    ....

3   What expectation might shareholders have of the acid test ratio at the end of the next financial year

    a) after the window dressing, i.e. on the basis of the two end-of-year figures on the diagram?

    ....

    b) if the window dressing had not been undertaken?

    ....

Workforce planning

A Missing words

Workforce planning means assessing future .... needs so that the objectives of the business can be met. This requires a forecast of the number and type of labour/skills required in the future (1–3 years, ideally); this should be compared with the results of an audit of current workforce skills, so that any gaps or mismatches can be identified. Where gaps are identified, either re-... is required for current staff or new staff will need to be .... If workforce planning is carried out with care, redundancies should rarely occur, as staff with skills that will be less useful in the future should be retrained and redeployed to new tasks. In reality, firms often wait until change hits them, instead of planning ahead.

B Management in practice

In a school the numbers choosing Physics falls each year, while Media Studies is growing. There are three under-used Physics staff and one over-worked media teacher.

1   Identify three alternative approaches the school's management could adopt.

    a) ....

    b) ....

    c) ....

2 Recommend one, explaining your reasoning.

....

....

C Data response

Look at the planning data below for Internetware Ltd.

Workforce planning data: inner ring is now, outer is plan for year's time

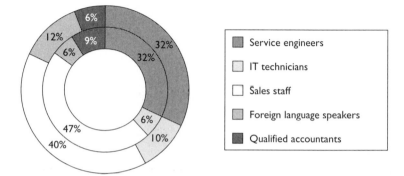

Legend:
- Service engineers
- IT technicians
- Sales staff
- Foreign language speakers
- Qualified accountants

1 a) Identify two skill categories where extra staff will be needed.

....

b) State a key assumption you have made in your answer to a).

....

2 The personnel manager has decided to invite four of the accountants to retrain as IT technicians or foreign language speakers. What difficulties might arise from this plan?

....

....

3 The total Internetware workforce now is 88; in two years it is expected to be 100. Calculate the actual number of extra foreign language speakers who will be needed over the next two years.

....

....

Examiners' Notes

Questions on this have been badly answered in the past. Remember that planning future workforce needs requires a) an audit of staff skills today, b) a forecast of the number and type of staff needed in the future and c) a recruitment and training plan to get from a to b.

Working capital

A Missing words

Working capital is the finance available for the day-to-day running of the business.

Much of a firm's capital is tied up in .... assets such as property and machinery; what is left is available as working capital. This is needed to fund the purchase of materials and to pay the wages, the rent and the regular bills i.e. all the direct costs and .... From working capital must also come the ability to finance the credit period given to customers, known as .... Working capital is sometimes known as circulating capital, as it flows through the business in a cycle starting with cash that is converted into stock, then finished product, then debtors, then finally cash again.

The formula for calculating working capital is current assets minus .... liabilities.

B Decide in which category to place each of the following items (tick one)

Item	Fixed capital/ assets	Working capital	Neither
1 Purchasing components			
2 Purchasing new company cars			
3 Paying bank interest charges			
4 Paying for extra machinery			
5 Paying the monthly salary bill			

C Which of the following formulae are correct?

Put a tick by the correct formulae in the following list

1 Current assets − Current liabilities = Working capital   ....

2 Fixed assets + Working capital = Assets employed   ....

3 Assets employed − Fixed assets = Working capital   ....

4 Current assets > Current liabilities = Negative working capital   ....

D Which terms are defined by the following statements?

1 Money owed to a firm for goods supplied on credit.   ....

2 Items of value owned by a firm for use in the short term.   ....

3 When current liabilities are greater than current assets.   ....

E Data response

Look at this balance sheet extract, then answer the questions below

	£000
Fixed assets	1,200
Stock	450
Debtors	260
Cash	90
Current liabilities	920

1 Calculate the company's working capital.

....

2 Explain two possible effects on the firm of this working capital position.

....

3 Explain two ways in which the firm could increase its working capital.

....

....

Examiners' Notes

For strong liquidity, working capital should be high; but for maximum financial efficiency it should be low. When measured by the acid test ratio, the number should be around one.

Revising

A Missing words

1 A price rise is likely to .... demand because consumers can switch to cheaper .... or may lack the .... income to afford the item.

2 A price .... on a price inelastic product will increase sales volume but .... sales revenue.

3 When sales flatten out within the .... phase of a product's life cycle, a firm should investigate .... strategies.

4 The .... Matrix analyses a firm's product portfolio in relation to market .... and market ....

B Calculate

1 **a)** The price a firm should charge on the basis of 30% cost plus monthly fixed costs of £42,000, variable costs of £2 and sales of 3,000 per month.

....

....

b) Despite this, why might the firm actually price its product at £19.99?

....

2 When a market stall prices strawberries at £2 per punnet, it sells 20 per hour. When it cuts the price to £1.50 sales rise to 50 punnets per hour. What is the price elasticity of strawberries at that market?

....

C Identify each of the following terms

1 A research sample drawn by picking every 20th person from the electoral register.

....

2 The degree of certainty one can place upon a quantitative research finding.

....

3 A product or business with a strong enough market position to ignore competitors' prices.

....

4 The changes in ownership as a product passes from manufacturer to consumer.

....

D Data response

Study the data then answer the questions below.

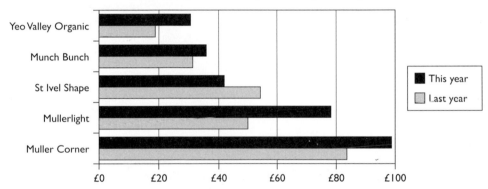

Sales of Yogurts and Dairy Desserts (£millions)

1 In the past year, the UK market for yogurt and dairy desserts has risen by 6.8%. Therefore which of the five brands seem to have gained market share?

....

2 Explain two reasons that might explain the sales performance of St Ivel Shape.

....

....

3 Why might Yeo Valley Organic be regarded as a rising star? What implications might that have for the business?

....

....

Revising AS Finance

A Complete these formulae

1 Selling price − variable cost per unit = ...

2 Demand − .... = safety margin

3 Profit = total contribution − ....

4 .... − actual = variance

5 Cash in − cash out = ...

B Cause and effect

Draw an arrow to indicate the direction from cause → to effect. Is the statement on the right the cause? Or the statement on the left? Or is the cause two-way?

1 Tighter budgets .... Falling sales

2 Falling sales .... Falling distribution

3 Higher contribution per unit .... Lower break-even point

4 Falling profit margins .... Falling sales

5 Lower net cash flow .... Rising cash outflows

C Twos

1 Give two examples of overhead costs.

   ....

2 State two advantages of using cost centres.

   ....

3 Identify two variable costs.

   ....

4 Suggest two ways to improve cash flow.

   ....

5 Give two disadvantages of zero budgeting.

   ....

D Calculations

1 Calculate the break-even point and safety margin if a firm has fixed costs of £20,000, variable costs of £3 per unit, a selling price of £5 and current sales of 12,000 units.

....

....

2 JB Co. has sales of 450 units at £8 each. Fixed costs are £1,800 and variable costs are £3 per unit.

   a) Calculate current revenue and profit.

   ....

   b) Calculate the new revenue and profit if sales rise by 10%.

   ....

3 What is the break-even point if sales revenue is £140,000, fixed costs are £50,000, total costs are £110,000 and sales are 2,000 units?

....

....

E Explain the difference between

1 Cash flow and profit...

....

....

2 Contribution and profit..

....

....

3 Revenue and profit ....

....

....

Revising AS People

A Missing words

> 1 Management by .... delegates power while keeping focused on common goals.
>
> 2 A leader can delegate authority but cannot delegate ....
>
> 3 A medium-sized firm with many layers of hierarchy will have a .... span of control.
>
> 4 .... means keeping decision making power at the top of the organisation.

B Leadership

Link the pros and cons to the relevant leadership style, by writing down the relevant letter(s).

1 Authoritarian ....   2 Paternalistic ....

3 Democratic ....   4 Laissez-faire ....

Pros	Cons
a) Giving complete freedom to staff may empower and motivate	u) Decision making may be too slow in a time of crisis
b) Staff who feel part of the family will be loyal and cooperative	v) A risk that unclear goals may lead to uncoordinated efforts
c) May be highly effective at a time of crisis	w) Individualists may find the culture stifling and want scope to show initiative
d) Likely to offer excellent training and clear career paths	x) Ambitious junior staff will be frustrated by working to order
e) Good use of delegation should encourage motivation	y) If decisions rely on consensus, firm decisions may rarely be made
f) If problems are discussed it may be easier for staff to accept tough decisions	z) Orders given from the top lack the knowledge of those on the shop floor

C Anagrams

1 To widen the span of control   RED GAY LINE   ....

2 Discussing before making a   STUN COOL TINA   ....
   decision

3 Management layers   HAIRY RECH   ....

4 The number directly under   CLAP FRONT, SON   ....
   a manager

D Data response

Look carefully at Darin Ltd's organisational structure, then answer the questions below.

Darin Clothing Ltd – Organisational hierarchy

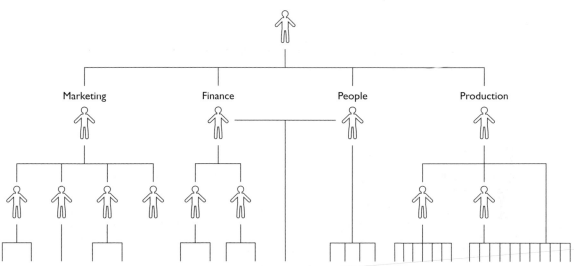

1 Identify three possible weaknesses in Darin Ltd's organisational structure. Briefly explain your reasoning for each one.

....

....

....

2 Darin's Personnel Director is keen to appoint a personnel manager from outside the business. State two reasons for, and two reasons against, this plan.

....

....

....

....

3 Over the coming year, the Production Director expects staff numbers to double.

a) Outline the risks of this to the business.

....

....

b) Suggest an appropriate organisational structure for the expanded production department.

....

....

Revising AS Operations management

A Missing words

1 Job, ... and flow are the three main ways of producing. Lean .... attempts to use the best aspects of each.

2 If output remains constant at a time when the workforce is being reduced, ... rises.

3 Capacity under-utilisation results in high f........................ costs per unit. This may threaten a firm's international c........................ .

4 The .... cost of a decision is the cost of missing out on the next best alternative.

5 C........................ .... measures actual output as a proportion of total possible output.

B Calculations

1 GF Co. has weekly sales of 7,000 units, a buffer stock of 5,000 units and orders new supplies once a month.

a) What is GF's monthly order level? ....

b) If its monthly delivery failed to arrive, how long would the buffer stock last?

....

2 James Gant Ltd has factory capacity of 5,000 units per week and fixed costs of £40,000 but the current recession-hit demand level is only 2,000 units.

a) Calculate the firm's capacity utilisation. ....

b) Calculate its fixed costs per unit at full capacity and at the current capacity level.

....

c) Briefly explain the likely consequence of these figures, if the situation continues.

....

....

C Which word is formed from the first letter of each of the terms defined below?

1 Desired minimum stock level. ....

2 The volume of finished product coming from a production process. ....

3 Carrying out different parts of a process at the same time instead of consecutively. ....

4 The collective term for raw materials, work-in-progress and finished goods. ....

Answer ....

D Anagrams

1 Comparing yourself with the best.   BE CHARMING, NK

....

2 Dividing a flow system into units/teams.   NO DTI CULL, CORP E

....

3 Reasons why small is beautiful.   DOOM IS NICE, ES

....

4 When stock falls this far, contact your supplier. LEER, RED LOVER

....

E Give two

1 Economies of scale.

....

2 Factors influencing the buffer level set by a firm.

....

191

3 Key factors in Total Quality Management.

....

4 Benefits from moving to JIT.

....

5 Diseconomies of scale.

....

Revising the economy at AS Level

A Which terms do the following sentences define?

1 The annual cost of borrowing money.

....

2 Accelerating price increases due to excess demand throughout the economy.

....

3 The account that shows how exports of goods compare with imports of goods.

....

4 The European single currency.

....

5 Willing employees put out of work by a recession.

....

B Calculations

1 IBM UK sells £1,000 computers for 1,600 Euros when the exchange rate is 1.6 Euros to the £. Then the value of the £ falls by 10% against the Euro.

a) What is the new exchange rate of the £ v. the Euro?

....

b) What price should IBM now charge in continental Europe, if it wishes to go on receiving £1,000 per exported computer?

....

2 Last year the retail price index was 281.5 (base year 1990 = 100). This year it is 287.8. Calculate the rate of inflation over the past year.

....

....

C Write out in full each of the following (all refer to economics)

1 RPI ....

2 EU ....

3 GDP ....

D Briefly define

1 The trade cycle.

....

2 Inflation.

....

3 Disposable income

....

4 Consumer durable.

....

E Give one good reason why

1 Firms with high borrowings like inflation.

....

....

2 Rising interest rates may push the £'s value up.

....

....

3 Unemployment may rise even if the economy is growing at 1% a year.

....

....

4 The job of a personnel manager is more difficult during economic booms.

....

....

Revising AS Objectives and strategy

A Missing words

1 .... are groups or individuals affected by a firm's decisions or actions.

2 Before trying to obtain finance for a business start-up, it is sensible to compile a business ....

3 .... are generalised statements of what the firm wishes to achieve; .... are more precise, measurable targets.

4 A sole trader's business finances are no different in law than his/her personal finances, therefore the trader has .... liability.

5 Profit maximisation is regarded as a ....-term objective.

B Aim, objective or strategy?

Put an A, an O or an S alongside each of the following.

1 'I want Fulham to become the Manchester United of the south' – Mohammed al-Fayed.

2 'Within this portfolio of 20 new titles, 11 are sequels to previously successful games and include *Who Wants To Be A Millionaire?*' – EIDOS Accounts 2001.

3 'The outlook is dependent upon a clear focus on short-term profit' – Peter Thornton, Chairman of Thorntons plc, in Annual Report 2000.

4 'To serve the world with style!' – Peter Boizot, founder of Pizza Express.

5 'The policy of recruiting young British players has continued' – Leicester City plc Interim Report 2001.

C Briefly explain why

1 New small firms struggle to get credit from suppliers.

....

....

2 It may be hard for a Chief Executive to find out all a firm's weaknesses.

....

....

3 A fast-growing company may not wish to float onto the stock exchange.

....

....

4 Good location is vital for most service businesses.

....

....

D Data response

The recession hit Jones plc very badly. The business had borrowed heavily to expand and now demand had dropped to below break-even. Colin Jones, the Chief Executive, decided he must look for staff cutbacks.

As required by the stock exchange, Colin announced a profits warning to the market, which included the solution

   400 jobs to go in Mountain Ash, a small South Wales town.

This led to uproar among staff, the local community and local suppliers. Yet Jones plc's share price, which had been falling, jumped up by 6%.

1 Why might there be conflict between the objectives of different stakeholders?

....

....

2 Suggest two approaches staff might take to persuade Colin Jones to change his mind.

....

....

3 How might the town be affected by these cutbacks?

....

....

Revising A2 Marketing

A Missing words

1 ....- led marketing focuses not only on customer needs, but also the company's strengths.

2 To make a scientific marketing decision, it can be helpful to work through the marketing ....

3 Comparing the relationship between past figures for advertising and sales shows the .... between the sets of data and may help in making decisions about future advertising budgets.

B For each of the following products, suggest a marketing objective and a suitable strategy

Product	Marketing objective	Marketing strategy
Limited edition Mars Bar Orange	....	....
The new £150,000 Rolls Royce	....	....
Hooper's Hooch	....	....

C Explain why

1 A reduction in price is unlikely to benefit a firm whose products are price inelastic.

....

....

2 A firm's long-term pricing policy may differ from the one it pursues in the short term.

....

....

3 A cow might be used to feed a problem child.

....

....

4 A sales forecast based upon extrapolation may prove inaccurate.

....

....

D Calculations

1 | Sales of Cardews Mint Chocolate have been falling by 3% a year for the last 8 years. Sales this year are 20 million bars. The management is considering moving to a smaller factory that will halve overhead costs. This factory has a maximum capacity of 17.5 million bars.

If Cardews moves in two years' time, what sales volume will be lost, and for how long?

....

....

....

....

....

2 | A manufacturer of footballs has sales of 100,000 units a month and fixed costs of £240,000 a month. Raw materials are £3.00 per unit and the pricing method has been to mark up variable costs by 100%. When it last increased its prices, price elasticity proved to be about 0.6. Now it is thinking of a further 10% price rise.

a) i) Calculate the effect on profit of this 10% price rise.

....

ii) State your assumptions.

....

b) List three factors that may have caused the price elasticity to have changed since the time it was measured at 0.6.

....

Revising A2 Finance

A Missing words

1 D... spreads the cost of a fixed asset over its expected useful lifetime.

2 The Net Present .... method of investment appraisal is based upon .... cash flows.

3 Actions taken prior to the balance sheet date to improve the apparent financial health of the business are known as .... dressing.

4 Profitability is best measured by the return on .... ratio, which measures profit as a .... of capital employed.

B Calculations

1 A £50,000 investment in a machine is forecast to generate positive cash flows of £25,000 for each of the next three years. The asset is then expected to be sold off for £500.

Calculate the pay-back period and the average rate of return on the investment.

....

....

2 Charit Ltd has fixed costs of £16,000 and is selling 8,000 units a month at £4 each. Average costs are £3.50 so the overall profit is £4,000 a month. Then a brand new customer offers to buy 2,000 units at a special price of £3 each. Charit's right-hand man – Daniel – rejects the offer out of hand, laughing at a buyer trying to offer 50p below cost price.

Comment, supporting your answer with calculations as necessary.

....

....

....

....

....

....

C Explain briefly what is wrong with each of these statements (from exam answers)

1 'They should use the reserves to finance the expansion.'

....

....

2 'To cut gearing a firm should borrow less.'

....

....

3 'A stockmarket crash may reduce a PLC's viability.'

....

....

D Data response

Harry Ramsden's Plc Extract from the Annual Report and Accounts

P&L Account	1999 £000s	1998 £000s	Balance Sheet 30 Sept	1999 £000s	1998 £000s
Turnover	6,833	4,888	Fixed assets	13,706	8,964
Gross profit	5,273	4,280	Stock	252	113
Operating profit	1,838	1,528	Debtors	3,229	2,388
Interest	318	192	Cash	103	75
Pre-tax profit	1,520	1,336	Creditors	5,911	3,873
Corporation tax	474	402	Net current assets	(2,327)	(1,297)
Profit after tax	1,046	934	**Assets employed**	11,380	7,667
Dividends	495	441	Loans	2,055	258
Transfer to reserves	551	493	Shareholders funds	9,325	7,409
			Capital employed	11,380	7,667

1 State Harry Ramsden's

a) 1999 earnings ....

b) 1999 working capital. ....

2 Calculate Harry Ramsden's

a) 1999 cost of sales ....

b) 1998 and 1999 gearing ....

c) 1999 asset turnover. ....

Revising A2 People management

A Missing words

1 Trade unions offer legal advice and support to members, and negotiate on pay and conditions through the process called c................................. b................................. .

2 Industrial disputes can be resolved by involving ACAS (the Advisory Conciliation and A................................. Service).

3 .... planning involves forecasting the quantity and type of labour needed over the coming months or years.

4 Productivity will rise even when production levels are stable, if .... is reduced.

B Match the factor to the topic by writing down the relevant letter(s)

1 Barriers to effective communication   ....

2 Communication problems for large firms   ....

3 Importance of motivation to effective communication   ....

4 Risks in excessive use of IT in communication   ....

Factors related to one or more of the key topics

a) Communication overload

b) Communication passes through too many intermediaries

c) Lack of a common language

d) Excessive use of written communications

w) The receiver may not bother to respond/provide feedback

x) Communication may be accurate, but too slow

y) Communication may be alienating if it is never face-to-face

z) In a well-run office, staff chat about key business issues

C Which theorist?

State which theorist you would use to analyse each of the following situations, and why.
1 A decline in productivity after a firm switched from piece-rate to time-rate.

....

....

2 The need to improve teamwork on the factory floor.

....

....

3 The need to rebuild morale and motivation after a bitter strike.

....

....

4 A department run by a manager who gives out orders and warnings in equal measure.

....

....

5 The need to reduce the number of graduate trainees who leave the firm because they get bored.

....

....

D *Briefly explain the business significance of*

1 Improved health and safety measures.

....

....

2 A company giving a union recognition.

....

....

3 Effective workforce planning.

....

....

4 Establishing autonomous work groups.

....

....

Revising A2 Operations management

A Missing words

1 Research and .... spending should help add value and support innovation.

2 The support facilities for a region, such as water and roads, are known as the ....

3 Computer-aided .... can help in developing excellent new product ideas.

4 Critical path analysis begins by drawing a .... to show the sequence of activities.

B True or false?

Place a T or an F by each of the following statements.

1 The critical path is the shortest sequence of activities within a project. ☐

2 Budgetary control, e.g. variance analysis, depends largely on spreadsheet software. ☐

3 Teleworking is working with the television switched on. ☐

4 Network analysis helps identify the earliest time stock will be needed, which helps in a JIT programme. ☐

C Circle the odd one out along each row

1 MASS   FLOW   BATCH
2 LFT   BSE   EST
3 CAM   EDI   INTERNET
4 R&D   TEST MARKETING   MARKET RESEARCH

D Calculations

Production:	40,000 units per month
Workforce:	25
Wage:	£1,000 per month

1 a) What is the productivity?

....

   b) What is the labour cost per unit?

....

c) What is the effect on productivity and labour cost per unit of a 10% fall in sales due to recession. State your assumptions.

2 Add the ESTs, the LFTs and the critical path; also calculate the float times for activities A, D and J.

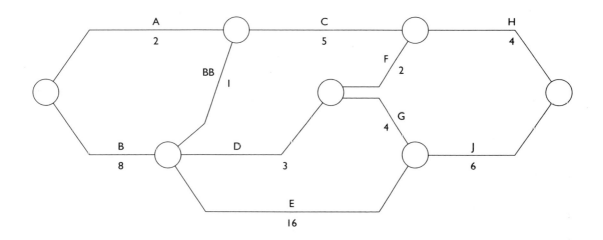

E Explain why

1 Efficient operations management relies upon accurate sales forecasts from the marketing department.

....

....

2 American and Japanese companies usually prefer Britain to any other location in Europe.

....

3 A good operations manager will always be in close touch with the personnel department.

....

....

Revising A2 External influences

A Missing words

1 A fall in the £ .... Britain's international competitiveness.

2 A rise in interest rates makes the external value of a currency ....

3 A rise in interest rates is likely to .... company investment.

4 The government's policy towards public spending and the raising of revenue through taxation is called .... policy.

B Anagrams

1 Government cuts £   A DONUT ALIVE!

....

2 Government interest in economic policy   Y POLICE NOT ARMY?

....

3 Average price level falling   FAIL NOTED

....

C Calculations

1   BJ plc has a £20 million bank loan from Barclays. While interest rates were at 6% the payments made a £1.2 million dent in the firm's £2 million operating profits, leaving profits before tax at £0.8 million. Some City analysts predict that rates will rise to 11% in the next year.

a) Calculate the effect on BJ plc's pre-tax profits.

....

b) Suggest two actions the company should consider to reduce its debt level.

....

2 If a British firm imports $1,200 computers from America and sells them for £899 while the £ = $1.50

a) What is the gross profit per unit? ....

b) What would be the new profit if the £ rose by 20%? (Assuming the firm decides to hold its UK selling price at £899.)

....

D Data response

Look carefully at this data then answer the questions below.

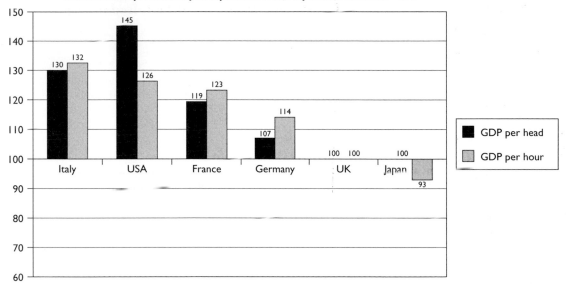

International productivity comparisons DTI, May 2001, UK Index = 100

1   Which is the most productive country on the basis of output per hour?

    ....

2   Suggest two key factors that may explain Britain's relatively poor productivity compared with Italy and France.

    ....

    ....

3   Japan's poor position is due to its poor productivity in agriculture and services. Suggest one way productivity might be improved in agriculture.

    ....

    ....

Revising A2 Objectives and strategy

A Missing words

1 .... Matrix gives an indication of the risks involved in major new product decisions.

2 Cutting back sharply on staff and factory capacity is known as r............................ .

3 A .... decision is one that must be made quickly or the opportunity will disappear.

4 Taking over a supplier business is known as .... , ... integration.

B Anagrams

1 A limitation you can't control   RELAX.NET

....

2 A merger between firms in different industries   RACEGLOOM.NET

....

3 Setting the vision out on paper   MESSMISTATION.NET

....

C Calculations

1 If there is a one in five chance of a new product succeeding in the marketplace, what is the chance of two consecutive successes?

....

2 Draw a decision tree based on the following.

A firm is unsure whether to invest £40,000 in new machinery or the same sum in a new product launch. The machinery has an 80% chance of cutting costs by £100,000 over the next five years; though there is a 20% chance it'll prove troublesome, in which case its forecast outcome would be −£60,000. The product launch has only a one in five chance of success, but that would yield £400,000. Failure would cost £80,000.

Draw the tree (use the space below) and show your decisions and workings.

D Explain what is wrong with the statements below (from exam answers)

1 'They could do an extension strategy such as a money-off promotion.'

....

....

2 'Horizontal mergers lead to lower prices due to economies of scale.'

....

....

3 'Overtrading happens when things go wrong when you're trading overseas.'

....

....

E Data response

The management buy-out was a great success for the first year. The culture of the new, smaller organisation was more entrepreneurial and more willing to accept new ideas (and mistakes). Then came a shock when the manager/owners sold the business to a much bigger, hated rival – making small fortunes for themselves.

1 Give two reasons why management buy-outs tend to be successful in their first year.

....

....

2 The motive here may have been greed, but why might the managers have feared their rival?

....

....

3 How might the culture change within the new, bigger business?

....

....

A-Z Answers

Accountability, authority and responsibility

A authority, accountable, responsibility

B 1 Responsibility must rest at the top of a division or an organisation. This is because the person at the top is responsible for the appointments below, and therefore any failures can be blamed on the boss. Nevertheless, the boss can pass authority down to those s/he trusts
2 If the chain of command is complex, praise or blame may be difficult to place on any one set of shoulders
3 Decision making power (authority) may be meaningless if the manager lacks the resources to put the decision into effect

C 1 Two supervisors have 5 staff between them. Who is accountable to whom? One of the supervisors also has one employee to him/herself; this creates a risk that the supervisor will concentrate on this person at the expense of the others
2 Can the director of Dept C have full authority, when the director of Dept B also has authority over one of the key managers in Dept C? In both Dept B and C it is unclear which supervisor is in authority over which shopfloor worker
3 Hard to say, as accountability is unclear at shopfloor level, and is unclear at director level

D 1 Often because the person at the top feels s/he has delegated authority down the hierarchy, but the manager in charge believes that the problems/risks are known and accepted by those at the top
2 Authority is decision making power; autocracy is when that power is kept at the top, i.e. not delegated
3 Yes, as long as the managers and staff involved discuss who is responsible for what
4 If there is a culture of blame (e.g. sackings for those who make mistakes) the employee may be unwilling to take necessary risks in the decisions s/he makes

Adding value

A £1.75, profit, selling price

B 1 c, d, e, f, h
2 c, e, g, h
3 a, e, h
4 a, b, c, e, f, h

C 1 a) £590 b) Because overhead costs have not yet been accounted for
2 a) i) £23.40 ii) 3,900% iii) £351 million
b) Overheads such as staffing, advertising and R&D may be very high; may claim that the profit is needed to finance the company's next product innovation

D 1 If there is nothing comparable, people have to pay the price charged as long as they want the item
2 Consumers (especially affluent ones) are willing to pay high prices for distinctive design

Aims and objectives

A goal, aims, objectives, objectives

B 1 a) quantified and with a clear timescale
b) i) and ii) only

C 1 Helps in delegating authority if all share a clear view of the future
2 May help motivate staff, especially if the aims are inspiring or visionary
3 Should avoid the business getting side-tracked, e.g. opening high street branches

D 1 A 2 A 3 S 4 O 5 O 6 S 7 O

Ansoff's matrix

A market, products, diversification

B 1 Because the attitudes and needs of the customers are not yet known
2 Because they are new, they will face less competition than more conventional products
3 Because this form of market development is risky, as Ansoff makes clear. British retailers do not know or understand the huge US market

C
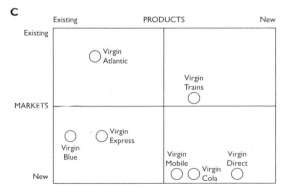

209

D 1 b 2 d 3 a 4 c

Assets employed

A Fixed assets, capital, capital

B 1 a, c, d

C 1 £130,000
2 £45,000

D 1 Working capital = £210,000
2 Assets employed = £1,310,000
3 Capital employed = £1,310,000

Average rate of return (ARR)

A percentage, outlay/investment, risk

B Advantages: 2 and 3 (4 is true, but not really an advantage)

C 1 20%
2 **a)** Criterion rate or criterion level; **b)** Net cash flow over the 3 years = £45,000, i.e. £15,000 a year. So ARR = 25%. So yes, the project has high enough returns

D 1 ARR indicates profitability of an investment; for larger, cash-rich firms, pay-back may not be an important issue
2 Pay-back tells you for how long your investment is at risk (ARR doesn't); forecasts of pay-back period are more likely to prove correct, as they don't look too many years into the future

E 1 F 2 T 3 T

Balance sheet 1

A assets, liabilities, time, capital, fixed, working, assets

B 1 creditors
2 old stock
3 cash
4 stock

C 1 fixed assets
2 current assets
3 current liabilities
4 working capital
5 long-term liabilities

D

Fixed assets	Property	£150,000
	Stock	£40,000
	Debtors and cash	£60,000
Current liabilities	Creditors	£25,000
Assets employed		£225,000

Long-term liabilities	Share capital	£10,000
	Loans	£65,000
	Reserves	£150,000
Capital employed		£225,000

Balance sheet 2

A 1 Creditors (others are current assets)
2 Cash (others comprise the capital employed)
3 Goodwill (others are tangible assets)
4 Acid test (others are expressed as percentages)

B 1 acid, liabilities
2 capital, used
3 gearing, gearing

C 1 **a)** 0.5 **b)** £170,000 **c)** 45 days; assuming the debtors figure at the end of year was typical of the whole year
2 £360,000 (annual sales at cost = £30,000 × 6 = £180,000; if gross margin is 50%, sales revenue must be twice the cost of sales figure)

Break-even analysis

A See figure below. Note: break-even at 2,000 units, safety margin = 225 units; £10,000 loss made at 1,000 units

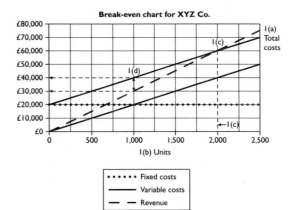

Break-even chart for XYZ Co.

B 1 **a)** £30 **b)** £20,000 divided by (£30 − £20) = 2,000 units **c)** £5,000

C That variable costs are always exactly the same per unit (which ignores bulk buying discounts); that the price charged is the same for all units (whereas many firms would accept orders at lower prices to use up any spare capacity)

D 1 **a)** Existing profit = £40,000
b) New profit = £5,000, so change in profit = £35,000 drop

E See figure below. Note: Profit = £40,000 and safety margin = 25,000 units

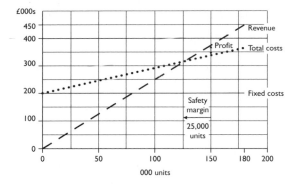

Budgeting
A costs, sales, cost, undershot
B 1 T
2 T (they want to make them easy to beat)
3 F
4 T

C 1 variance 2 zero budgeting 3 negative (or adverse) variance

D a) = £20,000 b) = (£15,000) c) = £5,000
d) = £0 e) = £0 f) = (£10,000) g) = £5,000
h) = (£10,000) i) = (£5,000) j) = (£5,000)
k) = (£15,000)

E 1 He *set* the targets, apparently with no consultation with staff
2 May reduce willingness to give time, effort and ideas freely
3 a) Crucial to find out why morale was low before bringing in a new system; b) must consult, and make sure staff believe in the targets they're trying to meet; c) beware of linking bonuses to budgetary success; d) remember that budgets can be a hindrance if they're too easy as well as too hard

Business cycle
A trade, market, five

B 1 C and E 2 C 3 E 4 C
5 E 6 C 7 E 8 E (perhaps C too)

C 1 Customers are reluctant to pay; falling demand may mean stocks rise uncomfortably
2 Because businesses and households take an unpredictable time to respond to economic stimuli such as a sharp cut in interest rates
3 Sharp upturns tend to mean dramatic downturns

D 1 b, y 2 c, z 3 a, c, d, w 4 x

E 1 Delayed orders may yet come in, if confidence returns
2 Postponing cost cutting probably means operating below break-even for several months, at low levels of capacity utilisation
3 They have been loyal, and if protected will continue to be so for the foreseeable future. Shareholders are supposed to be investing 'risk capital', so it is right that they should suffer (temporarily), rather than people whose livelihoods depend upon the firm

Business organisations
A liability, traders, incorporated, private, public, shareholders

B 1 T 2 F 3 T 4 F 5 T

C 1 c, d 2 a, y 3 w, x 4 b, z

Business plan
A small, hunch, cash flow

B 1 e 2 f 3 b 4 c 5 a 6 d

C 1 Time-consuming; new small firms may doubt their own ability to forecast sales with any accuracy
2 The business-people have every reason for bias in drawing up the plan; even independent professionals can struggle to predict sales accurately
3 May point to a financing gap that can be addressed by raising extra capital; may prevent under-pricing (one of the main mistakes made by new businesses)

D 1 F 2 F 3 T 4 T

E 1 Good as a working document; no good as a way of obtaining finance from a bank
2 Probably useless as a working document, but will have the technical detail the bank wants

Capacity utilisation and intensity
A volume, 65, overhead, high, small, service/tertiary

B 1 F 2 T 3 T 4 T 5 T

C 1 a) 90%; b) 60% (£2,400 as a % of £4,000);
c) Low labour costs per unit; but perhaps a low level of customer service
2 a) 60%;
b) £5 p.u. at 120,000; £3 p.u. at 200,000
c) As variable costs are £2 p.u., total cost p.u. is £7 at 120,000 but only £5 at 200,000. As selling price is £8, the profit difference is clear;
d) 120,000 × £1 = £120,000; 200,000 × £3 = £600,000. So the % increase is 400% (£480,000/ £120,000 × 100)

Capital and revenue expenditure

A fixed, lifetime, materials/rent/rates/telephone/maintenance and many others

B 1 T 2 T 3 F (if the raw materials cannot be sold, no revenue would be generated) 4 T

C 1 The value of fixed assets would fall, as would the capital reserves
2 A charge of £25,000 would be made each year (assuming zero residual value)
3 May reduce productivity, which would make it harder to compete on price
4 This would spread the cost over a longer period, boosting the book value of the robots and boosting capital reserves

Cash flow

A out, month

B 1 **B**ad debt; 2 **A**ssets; 3 **S**ale and leaseback; 4 **F**actoring. *Answer* BASF

C 1 Constant need to increase capacity causes major outflows; cash in from sales lags behind today's cash outflows (which relate to today's higher sales level)
2 Several months of zero cash inflow, during the credit period; this will hit cash flow very hard
3 Brings forward cash from customers and therefore gives cash flow a major, one-off boost

D 1 a) £5,000 b) £50,000 c) £90,000
d) £25,000 e) £75,000 f) £125,000
g) £100,000 h) £100,000 i) £15,000
j) £115,000
2 a) It will push it into the red
b) Obtain a loan or extra share capital; the seasonal peak period is nearly over, so it will be hard to finance the debt through monthly cash flows

E 1 Highly seasonal pattern of demand; takings also affected by unpredictable factors, such as whether it's a hot spring and summer in Britain
2 Unable to take advantage of new opportunities (can't finance them); high interest payments

Communication

A goals, customers, intermediaries, diseconomy

B 1 b 2 f 3 a 4 e 5 c 6 d

C 1 Low morale; lack of common language
2 So the transmitter knows the message was received and understood; to encourage two-way communications, i.e. dialogue

3 Delegating authority to cost or profit centres; delayering the hierarchy
4 Easy to feel alienated if you don't feel involved; rumours can spread that are worse than the truth

D 1 Messages sent through intermediaries can become distorted and therefore inaccurate
2 The only way she could turn it round would be to bring all 80 staff together, be open about the firm's difficulties, admit she's been under great stress, apologise, then encourage people to talk about how best to improve relations and communications

Constraints (internal and external)

A objectives/goals, external, pressure, constraint

B 1 E (or I, possibly) 2 N 3 E 4 E 5 I 6 E
7 E 8 N 9 I

C 1 Sell a fixed asset for cash to generate the funds (or sell off an under-performing division of the business)
2 Find out why they're leaving. Then, if necessary, offer better remuneration or more flexible working hours
3 May need to create a new, more youthful brand name, though this is likely to be very expensive, so would only be worthwhile if there were further, youth-focused products under development

D 1 c 2 d 3 b 4 a

E 1 Buy up that supplier or set up own subsidiary factories in low-cost, developing countries
2 Find component suppliers in the countries you export to (so that problems with export prices are offset by lower import costs)
3 Maximise your product differentiation (when *The Times* cut its cover price sharply, sales of *The Guardian* were unaffected)

Contribution

A variable, profit, profit

B 1 T 2 T 3 T 4 F (depends how much sales fall)

C 1 a) £1.60 b) 2, 500 units (£4,000/£1.60)
c) £5,600
2 a) Before: £1.20 contribution × 50,000 = £60,000 *minus* £15,000 = £45,000 profit
b) After: £1 contribution × 56,000 = £56,000 *minus* £15,000 = £41,000 profit
c) If the objective was to boost profit, they should not have done it

Cost and profit centres

A delegate

B 1 T 2 F 3 T 4 T 5 T

C 1 Pros: c, y   Cons: z
  2 Pros: c, y   Cons: e, w
  3 Pros: b, x   Cons: d
  4 Pros: a, c, y   Cons: v

D 1 short-term; 2 overhead; 3 responsibility

Costs

A variable, overheads/expenses, rent (delete components), number of units

B 1 variable costs; 2 total costs; 3 overheads

C See figures below

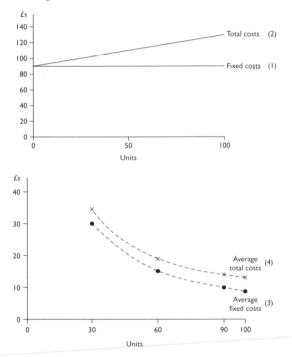

D 1 Fixed costs **2**, variable costs **3**, overheads

E 1 a) £1,800 b) 45p (£1,800/4,000 units)
    c) Sales are lower so overheads are spread over fewer units. Therefore costs are higher per unit.
  2 a) £42,000/1,200 = £35 fixed costs per unit.
      £35 + £8 = £43 average cost per unit
    b) £42,000/750 = £56 fixed costs per unit.
      £56 + £8 = £64 average cost per unit
    c) Profit margin was £22 per unit (£65 − £43); now is only £1!

Decision trees

A chance, squares, circles/nodes, probability, left, right

B Choice: 1, 5 (others are chance events)

C 1 2,600 (2,000 × 0.4) + (3,000 × 0.6)
  2 £34,000 (£10,000 × 0.1) + (£30,000 × 0.6) + (£50,000 × 0.3)

D 1 Node 1 = £570,000   Node 2 = £1,100,000
  2 Launch A = £170,000   Launch B = £700,000
  3 Can the firm afford to lose £1,400,000? Because launch B gives a 40% chance of that happening

E See figure below

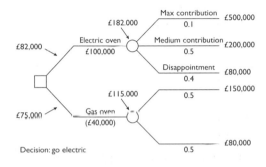

Decision: go electric

Delegation and consultation

A consultation, delegation, authority, decisions

B 1 D 2 C 3 N 4 E 5 C

C 1 A democratic leader would trust his/her subordinates with authority
  2 A paternalist is a parent-figure who cares about the 'family' but believes s/he knows best
  3 An authoritarian leader would give orders, not ask for views or delegate

Depreciation

A lifetime, 8 million, Loss, straight, (Historic cost − Residual value)/Years of expected useful life

B 1 a) £6,000 b) £13,000
  2 a) i) £24,000 ii) £72,000 iii) £82,000
    b) Year 3 depreciation charge will have to be £72,000 (3 years' worth, reducing the book value to £10,000) so the net profit will be £40,000 − £72,000 = (£32,000) for year three

Economic growth

A Gross Domestic Product, productivity

B 1 £15,583
  2 Higher labour productivity in US; higher capital investment per head in US; the country may be relatively richer in resources, e.g. oil, coal and agricultural produce

C 1 F 2 T 3 T

D 1 a) Appears quite similar, with growth varying between 1.8% and 4%; b) after allowing for inflation

2 Investment spending tends to be bunched into periods when business people are feeling optimistic and business profits are high; similarly, sharp falls in investment can occur when the economy is rather flat **3** It would know that consumers cut back sharply on consumer durables when the economy is weak; so the car producers would probably cut back production and stock levels

Economies and diseconomies of scale

A costs, higher, bulk buying

B Economy: 3, 5 Diseconomy: 1, 6 Neither: 2, 4

C 1 Bulk buying is implicitly something that a firm can only benefit from if it is operating on a large scale; every firm will attempt to buy their materials at low cost
2 Division of labour means chopping a job into different tasks, each done by one person (over and over again); multi-skilling means equipping staff to be capable of doing a wide range of tasks
3 Economies of scale suggest benefits from operating at a higher scale of output, e.g. a bigger factory, or from more factories; this can lead to diseconomies of scale; higher capacity utilisation, by contrast, can only be beneficial as fixed costs are spread over more units of output

D 1 Cardews: 5 tons; Planets: 7 tons; Nestee: 4 tons
2 The biggest producer has the lowest materials cost per unit, suggesting bulk buying discounts; it also has the lowest interest charge, implying financial economies of scale
3 The reject rate correlates to the scale of output, suggesting that the bigger the business the worse the quality level, perhaps because staff feel less personal commitment to the enterprise

Elasticity of demand

A 1 inelastic; **2** inferior; **3** high; **4** price

B 1 Inelastic; **2** Competition; **3** Negative

C 1 (–)4
2 £150,000 (3,000 units × £50)

D 1 price elastic; **2** income inelastic
3 advertising elasticity of demand

E 1 Revenue down; **2** Revenue up;
3 Stays the same

F	Rolls Royce	BP	YSL shirts
PED	0.2	5.0	1.5
AdED	0.2	0.3	2.0
IncED	5.0	0.1	2.0

(these are approximations; do not worry about being quite a way out)

Employer–employee relations

A 1 Kanban/industrial action; **2** Delegation/ways of resolving disputes; **3** Job rotation/ways to promote industrial democracy

B 1 Trade Union; **2** Sub-contracted or outsourced; **3** Works councils

C 1 Individual bargaining is when one person attempts to improve their working conditions/pay by bargaining with management. Collective bargaining is when a trade union negotiates for a group of people with a shared interest to further that interest
2 A team can work together under close management supervision; an autonomous work group has decision making power (and perhaps a budget) delegated to it
3 Conciliation is when an independent person acts to encourage both sides to a dispute to come together to look for compromise. Arbitration is when an independent person acts as a judge, to recommend an outcome to a dispute

Employment law

A parliament (government would also be a fair try), wage/salary, race

B 1 Working Time Directive
2 Equal Pay Act
3 Discrimination
4 Paternity leave
5 Unfair dismissal

C 1 Regulation ('red tape') hinders business enterprise and therefore threatens economic growth
2 Then multinational firms would decide on location on other factors, e.g. pay, rather than choosing the one with the slackest employment laws
3 High quality staff are always in short supply, so it is crazy to put some off by discriminating against them

D 1 b 2 e 3 a 4 c 5 d

E 1 equal pay **2** employment tribunal
3 repetitive (strain injury)

European Union

A tariffs, quotas

B 1 T **2** T **3** T **4** F **5** T

C 1 b, z **2** d, w **3** a, y **4** c, x

D 1 Withdraw from EU – to keep complete control of laws affecting our people; to escape the costs and bureaucracy of the Common Agricultural Policy
Stay in – to keep in with the region to which we send 55% of all our exports; to encourage our firms

to face competition and therefore keep prices lower than they would otherwise be

2 Join Euro – to minimise foreign exchange costs; and minimise foreign exchange risks (thereby strengthening our export trade

Don't join – because we lose important aspects of our control of UK economic policy; because we love the pound (not logical, but it seems very important politically)

Exchange rates

A $1.35, more, reduce/cut

B 1 They can't afford to push the prices up, because demand will fall very sharply
2 Because it cuts the cost of imports – finished products but also imported materials
3 A high pound forces export prices up; this cuts volumes and therefore profit
4 Because it will give them security from unexpected changes in the exchange rate

C 1 a) 96,000DM
 b) £32,000 × 2.70DM = £86,400 DM

 2 a) $11.10 (variable costs £3.70 × 100% mark up × $1.50 to the £)
 b) To benefit from higher sales below a psychological pricing point

D 1 fall **2** up **3** improves **4** high **5** European

Financial efficiency

A turnover, turnover, debtor, public limited

B 1 Assets (or capital) employed
 2 Sales at cost (also known as cost of sales)
 3 Sales

C 1 a) 2 **b)** 40 days
 2 a) 20 times
 b) Stock turnover has slowed. As sales have risen, the only explanation is that stock levels have risen faster than the 10% sales increase. This seems undesirable, as greengrocers want stock to be as fresh as possible. Stock turnover of 20 means the average piece of stock is hanging around for two and a half weeks (52/20). Dart Greengrocer's sales will surely not continue to rise if this situation persists

D 1 b and e **2** d **3** a and c

E 1 A risk of overtrading
 2 A risk of high wastage due to stock passing sell-by date

3 Cash coming in too slowly to pay bills
4 Inefficient to generate few sales from expensive assets
5 Customers may be upset and find another supplier

Fiscal policy

A objectives, taxation

B 1 **P**rogressive; **2** **R**egressive; **3** **I**ndirect;
 4 **C**apital spending; **5** **E**nterprise zones
 Answer PRICE

C 1 e **2** d **3** a **4** c **5** b

Flotation

A limited, flotation, shares, rises

B 1 Share buyers may realise the offer documents (the prospectus) over sold the prospects of the firm (as happened with the flotation of Lastminute.com); or the economic circumstances may worsen
2 To raise extra share capital; to enable the company founders to raise money personally, by selling part of their shareholding but without losing control

C 1 T **2** T **3** F **4** T

D 1 Divorce of ownership and control
 2 Short-termism

Gearing

A debt or loans or borrowings, capital, borrowed, interest

B 1 E **2** C **3** N **4** C **5** E **6** N **7** C **8** C

C 1 T **2** T **3** F **4** T **5** T

D 1 Yes, if it has growth prospects but the management is too cautious to borrow to finance growth
2 Because they have not yet built up reserves of accumulated profit to counterbalance any loans they had to finance their start-up

E 1 40%
 2 a) 50%; **b)** 60% (loans of £60,000 out of capital employed of £100,000)
 3 a) £1,400,000 **b)** 80%

Identifying a business opportunity

A patented, competition, copyright

B Correct order: b, f, d, c, e, a

C 1 There seems a lot of competition near by; and the closure of the previous business seems worrying. So, no, his optimism doesn't seem justified

2 Find the owners of the shopping centre Chinese, and ask about the pattern of trade, the type of customer – and why they believe the business failed; ask Don Lane customers to fill in a questionnaire to find out if they would use the shopping centre site, and what they would want from it (take-away only or a restaurant? etc.)

3 Chinese dragon 'event' in the shopping centre; advertising on bus stops in the High Street

Industrial democracy

A consultation, works, shareholding

B 1 C (true consultation, with full information and time to discuss)
2 L (this would discourage ideas and discussion; better to hold a staff meeting)
3 D (staff given the authority and resources to make a decision)

C 1 Could help motivate staff towards the best long-term interests of the firm
2 Gives senior staff an insight into the views and concerns of shopfloor staff
3 Provides genuine empowerment of shopfloor teams, i.e. true democracy (power to the people)

D 1 Staff like to feel respected, e.g. that their views count; involvement in decision making can break down 'them and us' attitudes
2 Staff will soon learn if their views are being listened to, but ignored; if, outside the works council, staff know a manager to be autocratic, they will not be fooled into assuming s/he's a democrat for one day a month
3 Groups find it hard to take tough decisions; group decision making is slow

E 1 Good decisions require full information from all sources; who better than the staff who work on the railways every day; a Works Council would have put forward the track engineers' viewpoint
2 If companies viewed this positively it would be excellent (this system works in Germany); the problem is that it will have little effect if it is forced by law, but company directors treat the worker as an outsider. As a personal opinion, I'd say yes, because if it worked just occasionally, it might prevent a safety disaster such as the Railtrack/Paddington train crash

Industrial policy

A roads, railways (or water, sewerage or schools) intervention

B 1 e **2** c **3** f **4** a **5** b **6** d

C 1 Heavy spending by government on industry (e.g. subsidies to keep struggling firms going) may be at the expense of spending on pensions or the NHS
2 Laissez-faire thinkers believe that there should be no such thing as industrial policy, because government intervention only makes things worse
3 Because of the social problems within under-achieving areas, and the problems of overcrowding caused by migration to more prosperous areas, many people see regional policy as the most important part of industrial policy

Inflation

A price, twelve, retail price index, cost, demand

B 1 Cost-push: b, c, f
2 Demand-pull: a, d, e

C 1 a) Inflation focuses staff on wage levels, as they are worried about losing out in real terms as a consequence of rising prices; industrial disputes are more likely when inflation is high and rising
b) inflation can also make it harder to forecast future revenues and costs accurately, and so may make firms more reluctant to invest in projects with long pay-back periods

D 1 a) down; b) up 2%; c) £10.14, psychological; d) expect, wages

IT (information technology)

A organisations, teleworking, budgeting

B 2 Electronic links enable you to find out your customers' sales, so that you can anticipate their orders (essential for JIT production)
3 A firm can keep local interest groups fully informed about any pollution accidents; openness in this way is a good starting point for building trust
4 Staff can be provided with access to key indicators of the firm's current and future position, e.g. weekly sales figures and the size of the order book; again, openness builds trust

C 1 Database; **2** CAD/CAM; **3** Scanners/laser scanning/bar-code readers; **4** Internet

D 1 Shorter lead times; accounts produced quickly; faster stock turnover
2 Higher staffing level, therefore can respond more quickly to customer orders; lead time may be a focus of company strategy
3 Improved knowledge of exactly what stock you hold means you don't need such a large buffer; if links to customers are stronger, demand can be anticipated so production can be Just In Time

4 Earlier warning of when things are going wrong; if you have longer between knowing the results and having to make them public, you can decide on new business strategies that will impress the stock market

E 1 Slow to respond; slow to develop new ideas (therefore never first-to-market)
2 Communication overload can swamp managers (all day spent on e-mails); e-mail can seem impersonal and therefore unmotivating
3 Good product design is a function of creative people, not IT systems; similarly, the best customer service is personal, not from an electronically managed call centre. (It's people that make the difference, not systems)

Interest rates

A money, demand, rise, fall

B a, b, c, d, f, i

C 1 Pre-tax profit down £160,000
2 Fall by £15,000

D 1 When UK interest rates increase, foreign investors put their money into English banks in order to benefit from the higher return. Thus the demand for sterling increases and therefore its value rises
2 When interest rates are high it becomes more expensive to borrow money and therefore more expensive to set up a new business. Also, when interest rates are high, potential investors may not have much confidence in the economy and therefore not want to risk starting a business
3 When interest rates rise, consumer spending is reduced (as mortgages are more expensive and consumers have less disposable income). So demand for many products falls and therefore firms may decide to cut stock. Even if demand for a particular product doesn't fall, stock may still be reduced because the opportunity cost of holding the stock has increased

E 1 T **2** T **3** F **4** T

International competitiveness

A high, service, price

B 1 Could result in an innovative product feature or process that would give Nissan a competitive advantage over other car manufacturers
2 Could enable Nissan to reduce its prices or to use extra profits to finance investment in newer technology equipment; either way, competitiveness improves

3 This could increase costs per unit and therefore reduce competitiveness; or it could enable a greater number of distinctive models (and special editions) to be produced, i.e. benefit from market segmentation
4 This would hugely affect the company, enabling export prices to fall 10% or – more likely – to boost profit from each car exported

C 1 Starting from a relatively low base; local labour costs are very low, so export prices can be very keen
2 High £ against the Euro; high consumer demand in UK focused firms' minds on the profitable home market

D 1 a) Middle management salaries
    b) Administration costs
2 a) Reduce wastage
    b) Redesign to use thinner, lighter or cheaper materials
3 a) Merge the two sales forces, cutting overheads
    b) Joint purchasing to increase bulk buy discounts

Investment appraisal

A cash, uncertainty, investment, pay-back, average, return, present value, 0

B a) Pay-back period is 2 years 3 months;
    b) ARR = 20%

C 1 Based solely upon the numbers given, the service centre should be chosen. This is because NPV takes into account not only both the amount and the timing of the cash flows generated, but also the opportunity cost of the money tied up in the investment. In theory, therefore, it is the single best measure of the value of an investment in real terms
2 a) Which fits better with the company's objectives?
    b) What is the company's cash flow position? (If poor, the packing machine – with its quick pay-back – should be chosen)
    c) Which has more qualitative benefits, such as improved company or brand image?
    d) Which causes fewer qualitative costs, such as reduced workforce morale?

D See table at head of p. 218. On this basis, Project A is preferable on purely numerate grounds

Just In Time

A buffer, control

B 1 JIT: b, d, e
2 JIC: a, c

	Project A			Project B		
	Net cash	Discount factor	Present value	Net cash	Discount factor	Present value
Year 0	(£50,000)	1.0	(£50,000)	(£50,000)	1.0	(£50,000)
Year 1	£30,000	0.93	£27,900	–	0.93	–
Year 2	£40,000	0.86	£34,400	£20,000	0.86	£17,200
Year 3	£16,000	0.79	£12,640	£30,000	0.79	£23,700
Year 4	–	0.735		£44,000	0.735	£32,340
Net Present Value:			+£24,940			+ £23,240

	Project A	Project B
Pay-back	1.5 years	3 years
NPV	+£24,940	+£23,240

C **1** Cut working capital usage; speedy, individualised production can add value
2 JIT relies on excellent communications and flexibility; it also needs high quality 'right first time'
3 May encourage a move from mass marketing to niche marketing, as a JIT producer can meet different customer needs with more flexibility

D **1** Cannot tell without knowing what stock turnover was previously, but it is clear that a lot still has to be achieved to catch up with the rivals
2 A firm with stockpiles of finished stock can deliver immediately; JIT production means you make it only when the order arrives

Kaizen

A continuous, Taylor

B **1** Problems in getting to know and trust new suppliers; lead times are likely to be longer if the goods are made overseas (especially Far East)
2 The customers could not switch their image of Iceland overnight; the company would take time to find high quality, reliable suppliers of organic foods
3 Productivity improvements require high staff involvement, not just capital; the kaizen approach implies improvement in all aspects (marketing, quality etc.) – jumping ahead in automation is not enough

C **1** No threat to jobs; not too much change at once, so easy to cope with
2 May generate new ideas to improve efficiency; may increase staff commitment and thereby motivation
3 Productivity affects costs per unit and therefore gives selling price flexibility; if competition is fierce, no firm can afford to slip back, even for a while

(e.g. prices too high for a year while awaiting new automated machinery)

D **1** New ideas for improving quality; higher staff motivation
2 Staff may have been reluctant to take the new process seriously; or managers may have been slow to implement new ideas
3 May be a new company policy emphasising speed of service, as a way of differentiating Page from its rivals

Leadership

A Autocratic, democratic

B **1** M **2** L **3** M **4** L **5** L **6** M **7** L **8** L **9** M **10** L

C **1** autocratic; **2** paternalistic; **3** democratic

D **1** e, g **2** c, h **3** b, f **4** a, d

E **1** Leadership is about priorities, a clear vision of where to go and the judgement to see how best to get there
2 Leadership is about inspiring others to achieve more than they could have dreamed of achieving
3 Leadership is about creating an environment in which people take control of their own destiny

Lean production

A waste, JIT, quality

B **1** Division of labour; **2** Bodge; **3** Kaibosh; **4** Just In Case; **5** High work-in-progress

C **1** **B**uffer; **2** **O**pportunity cost; **3** **O**utput; **4** **S**tock; **5** **T**ime *Answer* BOOST

D 1 Improvement
2 Cell production
3 Self checking

E 1 batch; **2** productivity; **3** fixed, overhead;
4 Simultaneous

F A is the lean producer, as it is much more efficient at stock minimisation and at 'right first time' quality. B looks better at 'output per hour', but what does that mean? If they have double the workforce, they certainly should have higher 'output per hour'

Liquidity

A cash, bills/liabilities, low/inadequate, test

B 1 Up **2** Down **3** Down **4** Up **5** Down
6 No effect

C 1 Struggle to pay your bills; risk that creditors may refuse to give you credit
2 Discuss with suppliers, asking for longer to pay; delay purchasing anything that can be delayed, e.g. new company cars or updated machinery
3 Improve profitability; scale down expansion plans

D 1 *Cause* May be stockbuilding for Christmas; *Effect* may struggle to meet liabilities
2 *Cause* Profitable, cash-rich firm with no investment opportunities; *Effect* may risk take-over bid; someone wants the liquid resources
3 *Cause* Its buying power enables it to finance itself by long (and free) credit periods from suppliers; *Effect* may prove awkward to finance itself if a price war undermines profitability

E 1 c **2** d **3** b **4** a

F If the business is investing heavily in new products or plant and machinery, its profits may be outweighed by the heavy capital outflows

Location of business

A bulk, bulk, secondary

B 1 F (mainly to developed countries such as Britain)
2 T **3** T **4** T

C 1 a, w **2** a, c, v **3** c, e, v, x, y, z **4** b, x, z
5 a, d, e, x, y

D 1 £500,000
2 Coventry is £250,000 a year cheaper than Derby, so it would take 2 years to pay back the higher investment in Coventry

3 £500,000 higher investment yields an extra £250,000 a year, so net annual cash flows are:

	£000
Outlay	(500)
Year 1	250
Year 2	250
Year 3	250
Year 4	250
Year 5	250

ARR = 30% (£150,000 more profit per year as a % of the £500,000 outlay)
4 May be more room for further expansion at the Derby site; the local area may have more availability of staff with the right skills (crucial, as the majority of staff have to be new recruits in either case)

Management By Objectives

A democratic, authority, objectives

B 1 *Invalid.* No, MBO should mean less bureaucracy as middle managers can make decisions without seeking approval
2 *Valid.* MBO is very difficult in businesses where demand is highly erratic, e.g. ice creams or computer games
3 *Valid.* This is a huge weakness, as easy targets are not only wasteful, but also unmotivating
4 *Valid.* This is the most important criticism of MBO. Bosses must always feel and be responsible – responsibility can never be delegated
5 *Invalid.* Of course, if the targets are too tough it would be stressful, but there is no reason to suppose this is a widespread problem

C 1 To give a clear sense of purpose; to have more authority delegated to you
2 To ensure that the objectives are tough, but not too tough – motivating but not stressful
3 Boss may not realise that serious problems are occurring, until too late; subordinate may lack the Hawthorne effect boost from the interest and concern of his superiors

D 1 Any employee can and should feel concerned about the ethics of this position. It is understandable to feel the MD is responsible, but the Sales Director is too senior to pretend the problems are not his
2 In a way, yes, because the MD may not have known the details of what was going on; but largely no, because he should have discussed strategy with his subordinates

Management reorganisation during growth

A flow, widen, layers, vertical, entrepreneur/leader

B 1 d 2 a 3 e 4 c 5 b

C 1 Managers struggle to cope with widening span of control; may be a power shift in the company to the people running this hit product
2 Management overwhelmed by constant need to recruit new, high-quality staff; can Coleman learn to delegate?

D 1 Span of control; 2 Delegation; 3 Bureaucracy;
4 Matrix management

E 1 Because of the need to delegate to new managers who may not yet share the firm's aims and culture
2 Because the self-belief, even arrogance, that helps an entrepreneur beat the odds can make it hard for them to trust that others have the ability to have authority delegated to them

Market conditions

A excess, cutting, monopolist

B 1 Duopoly; 2 Excess demand; 3 Oligopoly;
4 Free market

C 1 May be difficult to compete, with price competition quite fierce due to excess capacity
2 Shark may have highly differentiated products; Shark may believe that these actions will harm Broton's profits and cash flow
3 Predatory pricing

Markets and competition

A Excess, reduce

B 1 F 2 F 3 T 4 F

C 1 F 2 U 3 U 4 F 5 U 6 U 7 F 8 U

D 1 monopolist; 2 shortage; 3 duopoly;
4 fair

E 1 Unfair, because it is predatory, i.e. intended to injure the rival and therefore reduce competition
2 The bigger operator is likely to reduce the number of services and push prices up
3 Yes, to protect the consumer, though it would be very hard for central government to act on every instance of local monopoly

Market size, growth and share

A sales, volume, share

B 1 b 2 e 3 a 4 c 5 d

C 1 The average price level must be falling, which inevitably reduces profit margins (weak firms may not survive)
2 As sales elsewhere in the market must be declining, all firms will try to break into the growth sector, through new product launches or takeovers
3 Gives huge distribution benefits (all shops want to stock the market leader) and may enable prices to be pushed up; at the same time, bulk buying should reduce unit costs, so profit margins shoot ahead

D 1 Volume: 5 million bags (£16.5m/£3.30)
2 2 years ago 35%; this year 38.5%
3 Sales up by 25.5%, while the market has risen 3.1%
4 Darton's sales have risen faster (Darton's 25.5%, Lexington by 13.4%), but Lexington's sales have risen by more (£750,000 compared with £600,000 for Darton). Lexington has done superbly to build on its market leading position, but Darton can probably feel even more pleased with its success

Marketing mix

A strategy, price, objectives

B 1 b 2 c 3 d 4 c 5 a 6 c 7 b 8 d (or c)
9 a 10 c 11 b 12 c

C 1 **T**est marketing; 2 **R**esearch and Development;
3 **A**dvertising; 4 **D**iscrimination; 5 **E**lasticity
Answer TRADE

D 1 That spending on sales promotions may be more effective than on advertising (at least in the short term)
2 By identifying two regions where sales are comparable, then doubling sales promotion spending in one of the two areas
3 Because spending on sales promotions tends to be short-term, with little long-term pay-back; advertising is more likely to build a strong brand image

E 1 Might cut the budget for advertising; or might switch from spending on sales promotions to long-term image-building through advertising
2 Compare results with the targets set at the outset; use market research to assess the customer view of the new brand's image and to measure the number of buyers who are aware of the new product
3 Personnel may need to hire sales staff with experience at selling to higher class outlets, such as Harrods; operations may need to introduce stricter quality control procedures

Marketing objectives and strategy

A strategy, objectives/targets, Board/directors, objectives/goals/targets

B 1 S 2 O 3 O 4 S 5 S 6 O 7 S
8 S 9 O 10 O

C 1 If they seem unattainable, they will demotivate staff
2 Because it is the key to product differentiation and to repeat purchase
3 These are the decisions that have significance for the medium–long term, affecting everyone
4 It is vital to remember that the objective may have been impossible, or that circumstances (e.g. unpredicted recession) may have changed

D 1 Growth
2 Over-dependent upon one trend-affected product (sales could easily drift away); local managers may lack the belief in the company and its products that is a key to successful selling
3 Wrong objectives mainly, as it was illogical to build a business on such thin ice

Mission

A profit, strategy, statement

B 1 c 2 e 3 a 4 b 5 d (though the book on Richard Branson by Tom Bower suggests this is nonsense)

C 1 T 2 F 3 T 4 T

D 1 *Fail*. This isn't really a mission at all, just an objective. Therefore if it works, it is very unlikely to be a result of the enthusiasm and dedication of staff
2 *Succeed*. Certainly this has the potential to succeed in motivating staff, as there are many people who would want to work towards such a goal

E All three are very important. If pushed, I'd go for either 1 or 2 – eventually deciding on 1, as it touches on a key question – is it genuine or just for show?

Monetary policy

A Chancellor, England, up

B 1 Might stimulate consumer demand sufficiently to push firms towards their maximum capacity
2 Demand boost – especially for housing, given the lower mortgage rates – but also cuts the small firm's (probable) high interest payments on its own borrowings
3 When firms feel they have to cut costs each year, regular job losses can damage consumer confidence

4 As banks obtain a lot of money at zero % interest (from people's current accounts), their profit margins rise if they can lend out at a higher rate

C 1 F 2 T 3 T 4 F 5 T

D 1 Up 2 Down 3 Down 4 Up

E 1 Lower interest rates reduce the cost of borrowing money; lower exchange rates reduce the amount of foreign currency you can buy and therefore increase the price of imported goods
2 Monetary policy focuses on the amount and cost of the money and credit available to individuals and companies; fiscal policy focuses on the government's spending and its raising of revenue via taxation
3 Falling inflation means prices are rising, but not as fast as previously. Deflation is when prices are actually falling

Motivation 1. Theory

A productivity, turnover, movement, motivation

B 1 Herzberg; 2 Maslow; 3 F.W. Taylor;
4 McGregor; 5 Mayo

C 1 Z (other two are McGregor's leadership styles)
2 Pay (other two are Herzberg motivators)
3 Social needs (other two are key elements of Mayo's research)
4 Self-actualisation (other two typify Taylor's approach)

D 1 Social needs 2 Hawthorne (effect) 3 F.W. Taylor

E 1 To McGregor, there is no such thing as theory X workers, only theory X *managers*
2 Not if you take Herzberg's definition of motivation, which is that you are doing something because you want to, not because you are trying to earn a bonus
3 The hierarchy means that the most fundamental human needs are at the bottom of the pyramid, so you could say that physical are more important than social needs
4 McGregor's theory should be seen as relating to leadership, rather than motivation

Motivation 2. In practice

A related, options

B 1 **P**iece-rate; 2 **E**mpowerment;
3 **S**hare ownership; 4 **T**eamworking
Answer PEST

C 1 Because, as Herzberg says, low pay can demotivate, but increased pay is soon accepted as a right and therefore does not motivate

2 No single individual is likely to believe that their own efforts will have any significant effect on the company's profit

3 They may feel that they will have to 'carry' weaker members of the team; or may be too used to working in isolation

D 1 a) Little enthusiasm and productivity; staff complaints/'moans'; **b)** Poor or faceless management; too few motivators in the work itself

2 May help create more of a sense of common purpose; may make the work more enjoyable

3 Job rotation simply means swapping around different tasks of the same level of difficulty; job enrichment involves tasks with more responsibility and can therefore be more motivational

Moving averages

A competitors, moving, December

B 1 See table below

	Monthly sales	Moving total	Moving average
January	875		
February	1,250		1,058
March	1,050	3,175	1,025
April	775	3,075	935
May	980	2,805	1,075
June	1,470	3,225	

C 1 U **2** U **3** S **4** S **5** U **6** U **7** U **8** S

D 1 Must be 12 months, as seasonality effects would be very considerable

2 3-month averages would be very useful in the near future; note that soap powder has virtually no seasonal pattern of demand, so 3 months will be fine

3 If sales are highly erratic, 3-month figures are not sufficient (because any one month represents one third of the data, and so can distort the average); better to choose 6-month or even 12-month data

Niche v. mass marketing

A share, size

B 1 Mass benefits: a, b, f,
2 Niche benefits: c, d, e, g, h

C 1 There are a lot of competitors, so it is vital that your product stands out

2 Small firms are geared to low-volume production, using techniques such as batch production

3 Partly because they are less exclusive because they are plentiful; partly because they compete in sectors with many rivals

D 1 £8 million

2 It is £12 million of sales, so it could only be less profitable if costs were higher (very unlikely for a mass market product) or if prices were lower. The latter is highly likely to be the case

Opportunity cost

A decision, interest

B 1 Yes **2** No **3** Yes

C 1 Missing out on friends/TV/the pub
2 Reduced spending on education or road-building
3 Reduced finance (and management focus) for the UK stores
4 A larger overdraft, so the opportunity cost would be the overdraft interest rate (perhaps 15% a year)

D 1 Actual **2** Opportunity **3** Actual
4 Opportunity

Organisational structure

A span, narrow, bureaucracy, functions/departments

B 1 b **2** d **3** a **4** c

C 1 three
2 two
3 31.6% remains ($75\% \times 75\% \times 75\% \times 75\%$)

D 1 Damage to morale if redundancies occur; difficult to rebuild communication channels
2 Small-group, team communication should be very good; high degree of supervisory control
3 Can break down the divide between functions (therefore help horizontal communication); by the time people reach the top, they understand the whole organisation, not just accounts or marketing

Personnel effectiveness

A resources, turnover, absenteeism, safety, efficiency

B 1 T **2** T **3** F **4** F

C 1 Average number employed
2 Absent
3 Workers

D 1 Productivity up by 20% or so (good for profit). Absenteeism doubled (damaging profit)
2 Staff feeling exploited; staff feeling they need protection from poor working conditions

3 Apparent staff exploitation will mean reduced levels of experience and probably lower quality. Customers will be affected and market share may start to slip

Practical problems of start-ups

A break, cash, business

B 1 d **2** c **3** b **4** a

C 1 A location where there is a large passing trade may generate many more sales for an impulse purchase such as a kebab
2 Because no landlord wants to rent out a site to a business with a statistically high chance of failing
3 Helpful to know the demand potential (if low, can push for a very low rent)
4 With JIT deliveries, 100% reliability is crucial, so good transport links are more important than ever

D 1 Banks expect shareholder investment of at least 50% of start-up capital (here it's only 20%). No evidence of independent advice/expertise in drawing up the plan. Business plan may lack detail
2 Making customers aware the business exists; persuading people to trust the quality of the cars

Pricing methods

A objectives, penetration, predatory, taker

B 1 e, w   **2** f, x   **3** c, v   **4** b, z
5 a, d   **6** u, y

C 1 Loss leader implies pricing below cost in order to achieve market share (or sell complementary goods); penetration suggests pricing low, but not necessarily below cost
2 Cost plus is an ongoing method of pricing when there's little direct competition; skimming the market is a strategy for introducing a new brand, probably before competition has arrived
3 Pricing methods are ongoing, medium–long term approaches; pricing tactics are short-term responses to an opportunity or threat

D 1 a) Average unit cost: £8.20; with 25% added on = £10.25
b) £9.99
2 a) (−)2.34
b) Because price elasticity increases at psychological price barriers

Primary research

A quantitative, qualitative

B 1 c **2** d **3** a **4** e **5** b

C 1 A proportion of a target audience selected to match the profile of the whole market
2 That one can be confident that the survey results have a 19 out of 20 chance of being correct
3 A sample large enough to mean that the results can be treated with confidence

D 1 Starts with a question likely to invite rejection
2 Q2 a crazy question! (Likely to mean interviewers get slapped!)
3 Q3 is a leading (i.e. biased) question (implying that *everyone* buys organic veg.)
4 Q3 answers are meaningless; what does 'very often' mean? It means different things to different people, which makes it inappropriate in a questionnaire
5 Q4 has two questions in one
6 Q4 answers overlap (20% appears in two categories)
7 Q5 is a question that inevitably invites everyone to say yes
8 Q5 answer range is unnecessarily restricted (better to say: Yes, definitely; Yes, very likely etc.)

Productivity

A 1 worker, efficiency
2 investment, motivation/effort/morale
3 redundancies/redeployment
4 output

B 1 a) 350 units **b)** £50
2 a) 600 units **b)** £35 **c)** Vartex makes £9; the competitor makes £24

C 1 E **2** C **3** E **4** C **5** E **6** C **7** E
8 C **9** E **10** N

D 1 F **2** T **3** T **4** T

Product life cycle and product portfolio

A birth, maturity, competitors, tastes/fashions, extension, Boston, share

B 1 BM **2** BM **3** PLC **4** BM **5** PLC

C 1 dog; **2** full capacity; **3** rising star;
4 extension strategy

D 1 A (cash) cow has little or no growth potential, but generates a lot of cash. This cash is often used to help support a brand that is struggling, but in a market strong enough to be worth trying again
2 With its strong share of a growing market, a rising star could be a strong profit generator for years to come – so it's worth heavy investment today

3 New products take 1–5 years to develop (Sunny Delight took 3 years), so if you have left it until existing products are maturing, you're too late
4 Because they have no profitable future, dogs live until sales have slipped below the break-even point
5 BOGOF is a sales promotion (i.e. a short-term sales booster) not a medium–long-term plan

Profit

A sales, price, revenue, profit

B 1 £800 **2** £300 **3** £200

C 1 Despite the extra revenue per unit sold, sales would probably fall sharply, leaving total revenue lower. This would probably mean a reduced profit (though total variable costs would fall, too)
2 Lower demand would cut revenue and although there would be fewer units to produce, the fixed costs would not fall, so profit would be squeezed severely – perhaps even pushing the firm into a loss
3 A higher reject rate means a higher proportion of output has to be 're-worked', perhaps doubling the effective variable costs on those units. This will cut sharply into profit

D 1 Rent and salaries are fixed costs, materials and piece-rate labour are variable. At 24,000 units, variable costs per unit are £48,000/24,000 = £2. So at 20,000 units, total costs are (£2 × 20,000) + £72,000 = £112,000
2 £8,000

E 1 Because the fixed costs are spread over more units
2 Customers may not notice immediately, but in the long term they may switch to substitutes
3 Sales will rise, but perhaps not enough to outweigh the reduced revenue per unit (e.g. if the product was price inelastic)
4 Profit is a theoretical calculation (e.g. 'revenue' may be sales that have been made on credit, so the firm has no cash yet), whereas cash flow looks at a firm's bank balance

Profit and Loss Accounts

A costs, losses, corporation, directors, retained

B 1 cost of sales; **2** overheads; **3** one-off profits or losses; **4** pre-tax profit; **5** dividends

C 1 Spend more on advertising; employ more sales staff
2 Worry about whether this year's dividend can be sustained next year; worry about whether the firm will become complacent about overhead costs

3 When starting JIT, some late deliveries may cut revenue and gross profit; but JIT should cut overheads (especially interest charges and insurance on stock)
4 Exchange rate profits/losses; selling a freehold property for more than the balance sheet book value

D 1 a) Cost of sales; **b)** £1,050; **c)** operating profit; **d)** £160; **e)** £360; **f)** £90; **g)** £270; **h)** Retained profit
2 Low quality: because a high proportion of it is a one-off profit
3 No, because this sum is greater than the operating profit and will therefore be difficult to repeat next year

Profitability ratios

A margin, return, capital

B 1 d **2** e **3** a **4** c **5** b

C 1 gross profit/sales turnover × 100; **2** 14%; **3** 16%

D 1 T **2** F **3** T **4** T

E 1 40% **2** 33.33%
3 £100,000 (10% of the sales revenue)

Qualitative factors in financial decisions

A investment (or 'capital'), ratios, trees, pay-back

B 1 a, e, f, g, h, j
2 a, d, e, h
3 a, b, c, e, g, h, i
4 b, c
5 b, f, g

C 1 To remove a hygiene factor/demotivator and so help morale; avoid the chance of bad publicity from local pressure groups
2 Assumptions may have been optimistic on Investment B; assumed savings from fines for Investment A may have been too low
3 Seems more profitable than A; much quicker pay-back means shareholders' money is at risk for less time BUT: possible damage to staff morale from automation may damage shareholders' interests; local residents' campaigning on pollution may affect corporate image and share price

Quality management

A control, Total Quality Management, first

B 1 QA
2 QC

3 QA

4 TQM

5 TQM

C 1 BS 5750

    2 Benchmarking

    3 Self-checking

    4 Kaizen

D 1 a) Drake uses QC, as shown by the very high reject rate at final inspection; **b)** Mountain uses TQM, as shown by high customer 'delight' and high 'right first time' due to quality culture; **c)** Rally uses QA, as it has no inspection system; it relies on work 'right first time'

    2 high repeat purchase; word of mouth may boost demand; customer loyalty makes a price rise possible

    3 higher cost of materials; high training costs; heavy investment in modern machinery

Ratios

A accounts, year's, one to one

B 1 Smelly! Average fish there for one month! Should be nearer to 100, really

    2 Seems bad, unless the sandwich bar supplies local businesses on credit

    3 Fine, that's high, but the rising profits should enable the business to cut gearing in the next year or two

    4 Seems fine (in fact, at the time of writing it would be fantastic); key comparison is with the rate of interest

C 1 Use profit to repay loans; sell a division or under-used assets to repay loans

    2 Reduce buffer stock levels, e.g. by moving to JIT; raise cash by a sale and leaseback on property

    3 Sell off under-used assets; maximise sales from asset-base, e.g. shops that turn stock rooms into shopfloor space, and put all stock on display

    4 Cut the credit period offered to customers, e.g. from 60 to 45 days; or put more pressure on late payers

D

Falling profit margins ⟵	Falling sales
Lower gearing ⟵	Rising profits
Rising profits ⟵	Rising asset turnover
Falling stock turnover ⟷	Falling sales
Cut in stock levels ⟶	Rise in acid test ratio

E 1 Profit margins

    2 Gearing

    3 Asset turnover

    4 Acid test

Recruitment, induction and training

A Resources, Microsoft, induction, training

B 1 d, y **2** c, x **3** a, z **4** b, w

C 1 T **2** T **3** F **4** T

D 1 Helps line manager and applicant know whether they want to work with each other; but line manager may lack experience at interviewing

    2 Labour turnover is at its highest with brand new recruits; it would be silly (and expensive) to risk making it worse

    3 A chance to learn different/new skills; may help gain qualifications that help with promotion or – eventually – finding another job

Remuneration

A fringe, single, piece, Taylor, Herzberg

B 1 Performance-related pay

    2 Piece-rate

    3 Profit share

    4 Fringe benefits

C 1 Piecework reinforces behaviour, making it very difficult to get people to change their work methods; Herzberg thought money a distraction, leading to dissatisfaction not satisfaction

    2 May create 'them and us' divisions; share options may encourage short-term profit maximising decision making, to push up the share price (temporarily, perhaps)

    3 Pollution/congestion etc.; wasteful of resources, as company car owners have less incentive to look after the car than private car buyers (therefore may be scrapped and need replacing earlier)

D 1 c, w **2** d, y **3** a, z **4** e, x **5** b, v

Research & Development

A research, development, research

B 1 c **2** a **3** b **4** e **5** d

C 1 MR **2** R&D **3** R&D **4** MR

D 1 Because of the need to bring out new 'winners' to replace dying brands

    2 Because it adds value; affluent buyers will pay double for a well-designed dress, sofa or vacuum cleaner

E 1 b, c, d **2** a, b, f **3** b, c, d **4** a, c, d

    5 b, d, e **6** b, e, f

Safety margin

A profit, safety

B 1 **a)** 20,000 units; **b)** 40%
2 by volume: 30,000 units; by value: 30,000 × £4 = £120,000
3 **a)** 10,000 units **b)** 2,000 units

C 1 b 2 c 3 a

D 1 **a)** 9,000 units **b)** £18,000 **c)** £2,000
2 **a)** 25,000 units **b)** 5,000 units **c)** £4,000

E 1 To understand the relative safety of the firm's position; to help decide whether actions are needed
2 Cut fixed overheads; increase sales (as long as it's not too expensive to achieve this)

Secondary research

A size, share, desk, primary

B 1 d 2 e 3 a 4 b 5 c (NB answers for 1 and 4 can be swapped)

C 1 size 2 size, share 3 audits 4 Demographic (or secondary, as a weaker alternative)

D 1 Much of it is free in libraries; it is more likely to be objective (unbiased)
2 Often too out of date for fast-moving markets; rarely gives *precisely* what you want
3 Because *all* data should be treated with caution; because the market may have moved on

Shareholders' ratios

A gearing, acid, share, dividends

B 1 To support the share price, either to avoid takeover or to avoid shareholder criticism
2 A share buyer wants a comparison with other % returns on investment (e.g. bank interest), so the % dividend yield is very useful
3 If the yield is high, it is probable that the stock market expects that the next dividend will be cut

C 1 **a)** 30p **b)** 6%
2 **a)** 6p **b)** 5% **c)** £300

D 1 £400,000
2 No, because the trading (high quality, ongoing) profit was only £240,000. The only reason the firm had an after tax profit of £660,000 was due to the large one-off profit. Now the shareholders will expect dividends of £260,000+ next year, but the firm may not be able to deliver

Social constraints

A Chairman, general

B 1 **S**ocial costs; 2 **A**udit; 3 **M**arket failure;
4 **P**ressure group; 5 **L**obbying; 6 **E**thics
Answer SAMPLE

C Possible answers:
1 A; partly because exploitation *is* unethical, and partly because the company likes to portray itself as the consumer's friend
2 D; ethics are about doing what is right morally, not commercially
3 A; many human tragedies such as the Paddington Rail Crash come about because responsibility has been dispersed to too many people

D 1 They had received much criticism from campaigners and the media, and wanted to protect their image
2 Big brands have so much more to lose than firms with little public presence; so they take special care to avoid environmental disasters, and to know how to cope if something goes wrong
3 The media show more interest in covering 'events' such as protests; and governments seem more responsive to the media than to parliament

E 1 O, T; opportunity for our exporters, but a possible threat from theirs
2 T; most firms would see that as a threat
3 O and T
4 O, T; short-term opportunity to increase profit by cutting corners on health and safety; long-term threat to reputation
5 T; Long-term threat
6 T
7 O, T; opportunity (also a threat to any firm that ignores consumer trends)
8 O, T; opportunities for many firms, e.g. ice cream-makers; threats to others, e.g. heavy users of water

Social responsibilities

A stakeholders, limited

B 1 LSM 2 S 3 LSM 4 SM 5 SM 6 S
7 SM 8 LSM 9 S 10 S 11 LS 12 LM

C 1 Improves morale which may help productivity; helps in recruiting high calibre staff in future
2 Low profile means reputation may be unaffected by customer complaints; may lack the resources for the highest level of safety
3 Fear of takeover; fear of criticism by City analysts (who may call for management changes)

4 Brand image requires squeaky clean reputation; being responsible can be seen as a corporate luxury – it's easier for profitable brands

D 1 Responsibility to the environment (and to the long-term future of the planet)
2 Responsibility to customers and society generally
3 Responsibility to customers and to staff (who were being encouraged to be dishonest)

E 1 Impossible to tell without knowing the motives, but it seems to be socially responsible as well as being a useful unique selling point within the Co-op's marketing
2 Marketing strategy; Coca-Cola sees it as a huge publicity magnet that may help make Coke's image seem more sporty/healthy
3 A cynic would call it marketing; a nicer person would call it social responsibility; as with 1 perhaps it's both. (But if it's just being responsible, why shout about it as much as Body Shop does?)
4 Marketing strategy (of a deeply questionable kind, morally). If all the materials were unbiased it would be fine, but that is not at all likely

Sources of finance

A internal, external, share

B Internal: asset sales, squeezing working capital, cutting costs, profit
External: bank loans, venture capital, share capital, debentures

C 1 The bank can ask for their money back within 24 hours; interest charges are very high for long-term borrowing
2 Concern about public scrutiny (and the information competitors will be able to obtain, e.g. profit margins); fear of takeover
3 No interest has to be paid; it is permanent capital, i.e. does not need to be repaid

D 1 z (or, if necessary, a or c)
2 b, v or z
3 c, e, v or y
4 c, d, e, x or y
5 c, e, v or w

Special order decisions

A lower, contribution, revenues

B 1 a) £7,000; **b)** Increase it by £1,800 (£3 unit contribution × 600)
2 a) Before: £800 ([800 × £2.50] − £1,200)
After: £1,220 as the Tesco order yields 70p contribution × 600 = £420 in addition to the £800 being made already

b) Mr Tigana has been confused by looking at the average costs figure (£4). This is irrelevant because it changes when sales volumes change. The key thing is the contribution, and the Tesco order at £3.20 is 70p above the variable costs figure

C 1 T **2** T **3** F **4** T

D 1 Variable costs per unit = £2.50, therefore unit contribution = 50p per unit
Monthly contribution = £750; the 2-year figure is (£750 × 24 = £18,000) − £5,000 set-up costs
Answer £13,000
2 a) Is the 500 units of spare capacity sufficient for the next two years? **b)** Current customers are paying £4 per brush (£24,000/6,000); will they hear of the Egypt price and demand the same? **c)** Are there no ongoing transport costs to Egypt that should be allowed for? **d)** Will this order open up further opportunities in the future?

Stakeholders

A liability, shareholders, stakeholders, shareholders

B 1 Suppliers
2 Staff
3 Residents/the community generally
4 Shareholders

C 1 If staff become alienated the business may become less competitive; profit maximising pricing may alienate customers
2 Stakeholders' interests can conflict, e.g. increasing capacity may please shareholders and staff, but upset local residents, so total even-handedness may not work; decision-making may become too slow

D 1 Producer B
2 Producer A; making good profit, but perhaps at the expense of its suppliers, staff and local residents
3 Shareholders might want the cheapest solution, while residents want the best solution
4 Profit focus may lose staff and supplier goodwill, which may cause difficulties later on

Stock control

A minimising, maximising, buffer, fall, lead, Just In Time, buffer

B 1 Minimises stock wastage
2 A longer period in which unexpected changes (e.g. demand boost) may lead to stock-outs
3 (Should) give accurate, up-to-date stock data, so firms don't need so much stock 'just in case'

C 1 80 units
2 340 units: $(3 \times 80) + 100$
3 100 units
4 Demand increases sharply, causing stock to decline. The new delivery of 400 units comes too late to prevent being out of stock for a week

D 1 Any production problem can cause delivery delays; the same is true of delays by the firm's suppliers
2 Because the opportunity cost of holding the stock has risen; because the firm's cash flow may be suffering
3 Stock reductions generate cash; stock rotation reduces waste and therefore boosts profit

Strategic thinking

A Boston, Union, manpower

B 1 Yes, because it recognised the medium–long-term problem of their aging image
2 Yes, it was an attempt to reposition the business for the medium–long-term (but it failed, i.e. not all strategic thinking proves right!)
3 Yes, this was a very brave, long-term acceptance that the £billions spent by BMW on Rover were proving unsuccessful
4 No, it's just a short-term fillip to sales, with no long-term effects

C 1 b 2 c 3 a

D Crazy question! They are all amazing triumphs, but it will only be in a decade's time that we will really know which was the 'greatest'. Given the timescale, I'd go for Nintendo, which has enjoyed two decades of huge profits as a result of its shift to electronic games

SWOT and strategy

A Strengths, Weaknesses, Opportunities, Threats, communications

B 1 T 2 W 3 S 4 W 5 S 6 T 7 O 8 O 9 W 10 O

C 1 Strategic
2 Tactical
3 Strategic (but could be tactical if the intention was to drop the range after the competitive threat has been seen off)
4 Strategic

D 1 Might force them to think about weaknesses and threats; may help focus strategy on building up the strengths
2 Any information is only useful if managers act on it; Brian accepts weaknesses as facts of life, not as challenges

3 May have had experience of time wasted in planning for things that never happened; anyway, he seems too caught up in the new web-based software

Takeovers

A battle, intangible, shareholders

B 1 Backward vertical (buying a supplier)
2 Wal-mart/Asda is *horizontal integration*; though by opening up a new area of operation for Wal-mart, there are hints of a conglomerate strategy
3 Exactly the same logic applies for Stagecoach
4 Granada/Letts is a *conglomerate* merger

C 1 Merger
2 Hostile takeover
3 Goodwill

D 1 When an unwelcome, hostile bidder looks likely to succeed in buying another firm, a preferred company making a rival bid is known as a white knight
2 When the whole is greater than the sum of the parts, e.g. Firm A profit is £1m a year; Firm B makes £2m a year; but together they make £4m a year

E 1 False, the acid test is 0.3
2 True
3 True, Hassocks has a book value of £1.3 million (assets employed minus loans) so a £4 million bid is a £2.7 million 'overpayment' for goodwill
4 False, the bid is worth 80p per share £4m being paid for 5m 10p shares

Time-based management

A time, first

B 1 Simultaneous engineering
2 Lead time
3 First mover advantage
4 Just In Time

C 1 E 2 E 3 C 4 E 5 C 6 C 7 E 8 C

D 1 Customers may be willing to pay more; and more willing to order from you
2 Quick deliveries reduce need for high buffer stock; fresher produce/supplies
3 Speeds up the development phase of a project; makes teamwork and good communications essential
4 Cuts working capital investment in stock; places great emphasis on right first time, high quality deliveries

E Time-based drawbacks: 1, 3, 4, 5 (2 is irrelevant and 6 is untrue)

Trade unions

A members, collective, lawyer/solicitor

B 1 c   2 d   3 b   4 e   5 a

C 1 **D**emarcation;   2 **R**ecognition;   3 **A**rbitration;
4 **W**ork to rule   *Answer* DRAW

D 1 Good communication link with the shopfloor;
forces middle managers to think more carefully about
workforce views and needs
2 Membership fees of £100+ a year; may feel
compelled to join in with unwelcome actions wanted
by the majority

E 1 Delegation (other two are ways of settling
disputes)
2 Demarcation (other two are types of industrial
action)
3 Increase labour turnover (the other two are ways
of reducing labour turnover)

Unemployment

A recession, turnover, cyclical, structural

B 1 con/struc   2 con/struc   3 pro/cyc
4 pro/struc   5 con/cyc   6 pro/cyc, struc
7 pro/cyc   8 pro/cyc

C 1 Lower wages (or less pressure for rises); lower
material prices, if low demand is widespread
2 May switch away from image-focused media, e.g. TV;
may cut ad. spend to help finance price reductions
3 May cut labour turnover, so reduce recruitment
numbers; may cut need for high salary and bonuses

D 1 Little or no;   2 Boom;   3 Sharply worsen;
4 Slight fall

Window dressing

A shareholders, liquidity

B 1 c, z   2 a, y   3 d, x   4 b, w

C 1 F   2 F   3 T   4 T

D 1 May avoid problems with creditors; may avoid loss
of confidence among staff/players
2 Because outsiders only see the balance sheet
figures, drawn up on a single day

3 a) They will assume it'll be around 1.4 again
b) They might assume a figure close to zero
(threatening Chelster with liquidation)

Workforce planning

A staffing/labour/workforce, training, recruited

B 1 a) Retrain the Physics staff to teach media;
b) Make a Physics teacher redundant and hire a new
Media one; c) Hire a new Media teacher and redeploy
the Physics teacher to other useful work
2 Probably depends on your experience of Physics
teachers! I've known one or two who could be
retrained, though my guess is that approach (c) is
most likely to keep staff content while doing the best
thing for the customers (Media students)

C 1 a) Foreign language speakers; IT technicians
b) That the total staff numbers in two years will
not have fallen dramatically
2 They may lack the skills; they may look for jobs
elsewhere in order to keep using their professional
skills and qualifications
3 Currently 8% of 88 = 7; will be 12% of 100 = 12, so
another 5 will be needed

Working capital

A fixed, overheads, debtors, current

B 1 Working;   2 Fixed;   3 Working;   4 Fixed;
5 Working

C 1, 2 and 3 are correct. 4 is wrong

D 1 Debtors
2 Current assets
3 Negative working capital

E 1 *minus £20,000*
2 May struggle to pay its bills; difficult to finance a big
order
3 Selling fixed assets would generate cash; raising
extra share capital would also raise cash

Revising answers

Revising AS Marketing

A 1 reduce/cut, substitutes/alternatives/competitors, disposable
2 cut/reduction, cut/reduce
3 Maturity/saturation, extension
4 Boston, growth/share, share/growth

B 1 a) Fixed costs per unit = £14, so total cost per unit is £16; plus 30% = £20.80
  b) Just below the psychological price barrier of £20.00
2 A 25% price cut boosts demand by 150%, so the price elasticity is (−)6

C 1 Random sample
2 Confidence level
3 Price leader
4 Distribution channels

D 1 Yeo Valley, Mullerlight, Muller Corner
2 The brand may have been overpriced; the brand may have failed to keep up with the innovations introduced by rivals
3 It may have a very high share of a fast-growing sector: organic yogurts

Revising AS Finance

A 1 contribution per unit
2 break-even output
3 overheads/fixed costs
4 budget
5 net cash flow (just 'cash flow' is also fine)

B
Tighter budgets ———→ Falling sales
Falling sales ←——— Falling distribution
Higher contribution per unit ———→ Lower break-even point
Falling profit margins ←——— Falling sales
Lower net cash flow ←——— Rising cash outflows

C 1 Rent; heat
2 Helps to identify and control costs; may help motivation
3 Raw materials; piece-rate labour
4 Cut stocks; take longer to pay suppliers
5 Time-consuming for managers; bosses may not be able to judge the expenditure level that is really needed

D 1 Break-even = 10,000 units; safety margin = 2,000 units

2 a) Revenue = £3,600; profit = £450
  b) Revenue = £3,960; profit = £675
3 Contribution per unit £70; Variable costs per unit = £30; so break-even is £50,000/£40 = 1,250 units

E 1 Cash flow is the movement of cash into and out of a firm's bank account, whereas profit is a more theoretical calculation based upon assumptions and accounting conventions
2 The difference is that profit takes fixed overheads into account, whereas contribution does not
3 Revenue is solely the value of sales; profit deducts all the costs from the revenue

Revising AS People

A 1 Objectives; 2 responsibility; 3 narrow; 4 Centralisation (or autocratic/authoritarian leadership)

B 1 c, x, z 2 b, d, f, u, w, 3 e, u, y 4 a, v

C 1 Delayering; 2 Consultation; 3 Hierarchy; 4 Span of control

D 1 a) Staff in marketing department seem over-supervised; b) One employee answerable to both the Finance and People directors; c) Unclear accountability in Production department
2 For: new ideas; may need a staffing increase; Against: may demoralise current staff; new person needs time to absorb the workplace culture
3 a) Team spirit may be lost; communications will worsen; b) More supervisors needed; perhaps a new management layer

Revising AS Operations management

A 1 batch, production; 2 productivity; 3 fixed, competitiveness; 4 opportunity; 5 Capacity utilisation

B 1 a) 28,000 units (assuming 4 weeks per month)
  b) 5 days
2 a) 40%; b) Full capacity: £8 per unit; current utilisation: £20 per unit; c) The very high fixed costs per unit probably make it impossible to make a profit; to return to profitability a cut in capacity is needed, e.g. moving to a smaller factory

C 1 Buffer; 2 Output; 3 Simultaneous engineering; 4 Stock; *Answer* BOSS

D 1 Benchmarking; **2** Cell production;
3 Diseconomies (of scale); **4** Reorder level

E 1 Bulk buying; financial economies
2 Reliability of suppliers; predictability of demand
3 Should affect the workforce culture; should be built in to every stage of every work process, not just the end-point
4 Lower stock, so less working capital used; forces the firm to focus on quality
5 Costlier and less effective communications; less workforce commitment

Revising the economy at AS level
A 1 Interest rate; **2** Demand–pull inflation;
3 Balance of trade; **4** Euro; **5** Cyclical unemployment

B 1 **a)** £ = 1.44 Euros; **b)** 1,440 Euros
2 2.2%

C 1 Retail Price Index
2 European Union
3 Gross Domestic Product

D 1 Pattern of upturn and downturn in output and spending within an economy
2 The rate of rise in the average price level (but really the fall in the purchasing power of money)
3 Household spending power after deduction of taxes, pension contributions, etc.
4 A consumer good that will last years and can be used many times, e.g. car or carpet

E 1 Inflation erodes the value of the capital sum, making it seem easier to repay
2 Higher UK interest rates encourage foreign savers to buy £s to put their money into UK banks
3 Because productivity tends to rise at 2–2.5% per year

4 More employees leave to move elsewhere; a smaller pool of unemployed labour to recruit from

Revising AS Objectives and strategy
A 1 Stakeholders; **2** plan; **3** Aims, objectives;
4 unlimited; **5** short

B 1 A 2 S 3 O 4 A 5 S

C 1 Failure rate is high, so suppliers do not want to risk bad debts
2 Because staff may be happy to talk about successes, but keep quiet about flaws (especially if trust is lacking)
3 Owners may not want to dilute their equity
4 Because part of the service is customer convenience

D 1 Because, as here, their interests are different; the shareholders want profit, but staff want job security
2 Suggest that as recessions are temporary, the firm's long-term interests may be best served by putting people on short-time working, rather than redundancies; protest publicly to try to get shareholder pressure on Colin Jones
3 Severe effects on the 400 families, then knock-on effects as local suppliers and local service businesses close

Revising A2 Marketing
A 1 Asset; **2** model; **3** correlation

B See table at foot of page

C 1 Sales will rise, but too little to outweigh the lost revenue per unit (from cutting the price)
2 Long-term strategy may be skimming (high price), but short-term tactics may require a price promotion, e.g. when a new rival product is launched
3 A cash cow is profitable but has no future growth prospects, so the cash could be diverted to help revive a struggling new brand in a growth sector

Product	Marketing objective	Marketing strategy
Limited edition Mars Bar Orange	To boost total Mars Bar sales by 20% over the period of the Limited edition offer	Heavy promotion at the start, but focused on ordinary Mars, with the Orange version just getting a mention
The new £150,000 Rolls Royce	To achieve product awareness among all those considering a purchase of a £100,000+ car.	Achieving strong coverage within key media such as the *Financial Times*, plus a presence at events such as Royal Ascot
Hooper's Hooch	To restore the brand's credibility among 18–29 year olds	Redesign packaging and advertising to emphasise the adult focus of the brand

4 The underlying conditions affecting demand may change, e.g. before and after the 11/9/01 World Trade Centre disaster

D 1 Assuming the 3% sales decline continues, sales will be: next year 19.4 m, Yr 2 18.8 m, Yr 3 18.25 m, Yr 4 17.7 m, Yr 5 17.17 m. As the new factory will open at the start of Yr 3, 0.75 m bars will be lost in that year and 0.2m lost in the following year. By Yr 5, demand will have fallen to within the 17.5 m capacity

    2 a) i) Profit before the price rise is £60,000. After, it will be £98,400. (New price £6.60, new volume: 94,000 units)

        ii) Assuming variable costs stay at £3.00, and that price elasticity is still 0.6

    b) New competitors; economic change, e.g. recession; the brand becoming more, or less, fashionable

Revising A2 Finance

A 1 Depreciation; **2** Value, discounting; **3** window; **4** capital, percentage

B 1 Pay-back = 2 years; ARR = 17% (average annual profit of £8,500 as a percentage of £50,000)

2 This special order will boost profit by £3,000, i.e. 75%. Proof: when selling 8,000 units, total costs are 8,000 × £3.50 = £28,000, so total variable costs are £12,000 and variable costs per unit are £1.50. Therefore there is an extra £1.50 contribution × 2,000 units = £3,000 additional contribution and therefore profit. (NB this is hard; try the Special order decision questions, then try this again.)

C 1 Reserves are accumulated, retained profit; usually these will already have been invested; financing expansion requires cash, or ways of raising cash; reserves are not cash

2 Yes, of course, but how? To cut gearing, you may need to sell assets to repay loans or need to use new trading profits for the same purpose

3 Many candidates think that shareholders can 'withdraw' their investment by selling their shares, and assume that the firm will therefore have a cash shortage. This is wrong, shareholders sell their shares to others (through the stock exchange), so company finances are not affected directly

D 1 a) 1999 earnings (profit after tax): £1,046,000;

    b) 1999 working capital (net current assets): (£2,327,000)

2 a) £1,560,000 (the difference between turnover and gross profit)

    b) 1998 = 3.4%; 1999 = 18.1%

    c) 0.60 (6,833/11,380)

Revising A2 People management

A 1 collective bargaining; **2** Arbitration; **3** Workforce (or manpower); **4** employment

B 1 a, b, c, d, w, y

    2 a, b, d, w, x, y

    3 w, z (perhaps y as well)

    4 a, d, y, z

C 1 Herzberg, as his views on job enrichment could help replace the previous financial incentives

2 Mayo, as his Hawthorne experiments focused on this type of human relations management

3 Mayo again, as this calls for good human relations, with managers working hard to rebuild trust (though Herzberg warns that 'remembered pain' can lead to 'revenge psychology')

4 McGregor's Theory X and Y would be appropriate, as this manager sounds locked in Theory X thinking

5 Again, Herzberg is highly relevant; his focus on job enrichment might overcome the boredom

D 1 Can remove potential sources of dissatisfaction (i.e. hygiene factors)

2 This empowers the union within the workplace, which may help generate better two-way communications between management and workforce

3 Can ensure that the right number of staff with the right skills are available to help meet the firm's objectives

4 This form of empowerment may lead to significant improvements in the morale and performance of staff

Revising A2 Operations management

A 1 Development; **2** infrastructure; **3** Design; **4** network

B 1 F **2** T (in the modern world) **3** F! **4** T

C 1 Batch; **2** BSE! **3** CAM (other two are forms of communication); **4** R&D

D 1 a) 1,600 units per worker per month

    b) 62.5p per unit

    c) If no staff are made redundant (1st assumption), productivity will fall 10% and labour costs per unit rise 10%; but as people leave through natural wastage (e.g. retirement) the situation will improve

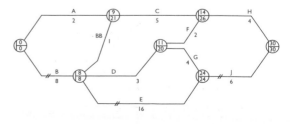

2 Floats: A = 19; D = 9; J = 0

E 1 To order the right quantities of materials and components, and to ensure there's sufficient capacity
2 We speak the 'right' language and have great international air travel connections
3 Ops knows the number and type of staff needed; personnel can recruit and train them

Revising A2 External influences

A 1 strengthens/improves
2 rise/strengthen
3 reduce/depress
4 fiscal

B 1 Devaluation; **2** Monetary policy; **3** Deflation

C 1 a) Extra £1m interest bill will push the firm into a £200,000 loss
  b) Selling under-utilised assets; raising extra share capital, e.g. a rights issue
2 a) £99
  b) £ = $1.80, so the computer now costs £667, so the profit jumps to £232

D 1 Italy
2 Poorer educational standards may restrict efficiency; poorer management: too autocratic in Britain
3 Merging farms may enable higher productivity through mechanisation (more machines/fewer people)

Revising A2 Objectives and strategy

A 1 Ansoff's; **2** rationalisation; **3** tactical;
4 backward, vertical

B 1 External (constraint); **2** Conglomerate;
3 Mission statement

C 1 1 in 25, i.e. 4%
2 See diagram below

D 1 An extension strategy is a medium- to long-term plan for extending a product's profitable life span; a money-off promotion is a short-term tactic for boosting sales
2 They may lead to lower costs, but firms would not pass those cost cuts on as price cuts unless competition forced them to
3 Overtrading is growing too rapidly for your capital base (and therefore suffering cash flow problems); it is nothing to do with trading overseas

E 1 New leader/managers are especially keen to succeed; past waste can easily be cut by managers who know the business
2 If the MBO is quite small and perhaps quite highly geared compared with its rival, the managers may be concerned about whether the capital they invested is safe
3 Perhaps more bureaucratic, with a weaker sense of team spirit and pride in the job and in the business.

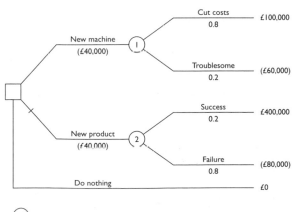

① £80,000 + (£12,000) = £68,000, i.e. £28,000 net

② £80,000 + (£64,000) = £16,000, i.e. (£24,000) net